The Essential
Staughton Lynd

The Essential Staughton Lynd

EDITED BY

WALTER HOWARD

iUniverse, Inc.
Bloomington

The Essential Staughton Lynd

iUniverse books may be ordered through booksellers or by contacting:

iUniverse
1663 Liberty Drive
Bloomington, IN 47403
www.iuniverse.com
1-800-Authors (1-800-288-4677)

Because of the dynamic nature of the Internet, any web addresses or links contained in this book may have changed since publication and may no longer be valid. The views expressed in this work are solely those of the author and do not necessarily reflect the views of the publisher, and the publisher hereby disclaims any responsibility for them.

Any people depicted in stock imagery provided by Thinkstock are models, and such images are being used for illustrative purposes only.
Certain stock imagery © Thinkstock.

ISBN: 978-1-4759-9332-5 (sc)
ISBN: 978-1-4759-9333-2 (ebk)

Printed in the United States of America

iUniverse rev. date: 05/29/2013

Contents

Dedicated to
two hard-working coal miners,
my father and grandfather:
Lowell Howard, Sr. and Walter Howard

Preface

Walt Howard's Introduction is abundantly generous.

At the same time, something rings true in his calling the pieces selected for this volume the "essential" Staughton Lynd.

My essential self is still the little boy whom Sam Levinger carried on his shoulders in a gigantic May Day parade in New York City. I am still the same person who precipitously left Harvard after reading Leon Trotsky's *Literature and Revolution*, which said that in the future socialist society all human beings would be Aristotles or Goethes "and beyond these new peaks will rise." I haven't found the revolution for which Trotsky called but I did find Rosa Luxemburg's pamphlet on the general strike. I am still the New Left administrator-for-a-summer who considers the Mississippi Freedom Schools perhaps the most important political experience of my life.

While living in Chicago I became friends with Stan Weir and John Sargent, who turned my understanding of the labor movement upside down. In Youngstown, Ohio, near which my wife Alice and I have lived for thirty-seven years, I got to know other latter-day Tom Paines: Ed Mann, John Barbero, and Marty Glaberman.

Finally, in my second professional identity as a lawyer I keep fighting for the "Lucasville Five," sentenced to death for their alleged leadership roles in an Ohio prison uprising. They exemplify solidarity across skin color and challenge those of us outside the bars to do likewise.

Staughton Lynd. May 2013

Acknowledgements

I thank Professor Staughton Lynd for providing me with the unpublished scholarly papers that are this book. I express gratitude for his permission to use the material he authored.

Editor's Introduction

by Walter T. Howard

As a collection of original, unpublished essays, this book focuses on one of America's greatest historians: Staughton Lynd. "The essential" Professor Lynd is the existential hero known as a "guerrilla historian" committed to social justice, political activism and building a better world. What is *essential* about this legendary historian-activist? What are his fundamental and key positions? The essays in this collection clearly answer these questions. In fact, this book is an edited collection of Staughton Lynd's texts over a wide range of issues as a moral model of scholarly activism. They are all here: Lynd's autobiographical analysis of his personal evolution as a guerrilla historian dedicated to radical social change, his revealing evaluation of his comrade Howard Zinn, his work with his wife and partner Alice in defending human rights in the American prison system, and their life-long practice of "accompaniment" as activists who became companions with the poor and oppressed.

The Origins of a Guerrilla Historian from Appalachia

A graduate student in American history at Florida State University (FSU) toward the end of the 1970s, I warmly recollect connecting with my advisor, Neil Betten, the specialist in Labor and Urban History, by way of our mutual admiration for the inspirational Staughton Lynd. Neil is the son of union activists, and I am a proud son of Appalachia and the descendent of peace-loving coal miners. At one of our first meetings, I smiled with an earnest heart as Betten and I both realized that we shared Lynd's social democratic principles and both believed in the sincerity and influence of his life and work. In due course,

Professor Betten launched me as a new Ph.D. into the academic realm to spread the Lynd gospel of non-violent radical change based on participatory democracy.

A descendent of Eastern Kentucky coal miners and United Mine Workers [UMW] activists, an Appalachian "Norman Pollack populist" by temperament, and a humble graduate of FSU's Ph.D. program in history, I found myself professionally drawn to Lynd more than Eugene Genovese or even Christopher Lasch, both of whom I have great respect for. Moreover, like historian Herbert Gutman, by the late 1970s, I already considered the Consensus School of historiography hopelessly outdated.

A young aspiring historian of that day, I was excited by the possibilities of history "from the bottom up," and encouraging the growth of a social conscience among my students. As a Lynd enthusiast, over the decades since those conversations with my FSU advisor in the Seventies, I have taught innumerable U.S. history survey classes and many upper division courses in Labor, Social, and African American history, to hundreds, perhaps several thousand, of ordinary college students from Middle America at five different institutions of higher learning from Florida to Pennsylvania. I have even taught history to federal inmates in the prisons of Lewisburg and Allenwood, Pennsylvania until Bill Clinton and the Democratic Congress ended Pell Grants for federal inmates in 1994. After over thirty years in the trenches of American college classrooms, my countless Lynd-oriented courses and political activism are a *fait accompli*. Things cannot be changed. In this regard, to a considerable extent, Omar Khayyám's "moving finger" trumps the lunacy and dribble of David Horowitz, Lynne Cheney, and all the representatives of the New Right and conservative talk radio, at least in the case of my academic career at the grassroots level of higher education.

My coal mining grandfather, and name-sake, who had little formal education, and who was as much my mentor as Lynd and Betten, taught me important lessons as to a thinking man's moral and social responsibilities in a democratic society. This mentor from my working class family, a UMW and CIO organizer from the 1930s, undoubtedly grins from his grave as I try my best to fulfill this responsibility through human rights scholarship that gives voice to powerless, marginalized groups. I would email country music bard Merle Travis

("Sixteen Tons") about this state of affairs if he still walked the earth; it would make a great coal miner folk song. Interestingly enough, near the end of his life in the mid-1960s, my miner grandfather told me that he wished someone would go to North Vietnam and talk to its leaders and tell them that some of the working class coal miners in America, who were not Communists, wanted to use common sense and settle the Vietnam conflict without prolonged violent conflict. This conversation took place in the "holler" known as "Bailey Branch" near Wooton, in Appalachian Kentucky, in 1965.

I was overcome with a feeling of serendipity when Lynd once informed me that during my grandfather's lifetime, he hitched-hiked through Kentucky coal country and witnessed up close the poverty and deprivation of its hard-working people. In 2013, in my current scholarly endeavors, he and my grandfather cross paths again. There is more: in the Freedom Summer of 1964, when Lynd was at Miami University in Oxford, Ohio, at the time of the tragic Klan assassination of civil rights workers Schwerner, Chaney, and Goodman, I was a hillbilly child and Appalachian-in-exile student in the public school system of Hamilton, Ohio, a landing place of many Appalachian coal mining migrant families, just twenty minutes away from Professor Lynd.

With this industrial Appalachian background, I have looked forward to honoring a mentor and inspiration. Having met Lynd several times over the years as a professional historian, I have enormous respect for him. In my long, unlikely and modest intellectual journey from Wooton, Kentucky to Bloomsburg University in Pennsylvania, Lynd has been a key figure in shaping my professional identity. My trek as a working class teacher-scholar from the "hollers" of Eastern Kentucky to the halls of academia drew direction and inspiration from this particular New Left lion.

It is also from such an authentic working class American perspective that I examine this important scholar who descends from academic royalty. If truth be told, I say with certainty, Lynd's life and example resonates with some rebellious, restless and discontented Eastern Kentucky coal miners and their sons and grandsons, as well as a few FSU history Ph.Ds. More than a few coal miners from Appalachia, and their descendants, would appreciate Lynd's defiance of Cold War authority and his distaste for the limited effectiveness of "corporate liberalism." Like the Appalachian miners, Lynd is fearless in his moral and political convictions. A careful observer can detect Lynd's authentic radicalism not only in his actions but also in his demeanor and carriage; indeed, in the very distinct way he walks and talks. There is an existential (Heideggerian) maxim of poet William Butler Yeats that "Man can embody truth, but he cannot know it." I have myself witnessed this phenomenon in regard to Lynd several times at various conferences and basement meetings. In 2013, as an over-worked history professor, I try to convey a Lynd-like "Weltanschauung" and hopeful social democratic vision of the future to about 150 college students every semester. Indeed, I have done so for over thirty years.

New Left History: A 21st Century Work-in-Progress

Several scholars of the American Left classify Lynd as one of the historians who epitomizes the finest qualities of the New Left in the second half of the twentieth century, and early 21st century. In his recent biography, *The Admirable Radical,* Carl Mirra advances a complex and nuanced handling of Van Gosse's relevant "declension" theory in analyzing Lynd and the New Left, it is nonetheless true that this New Left legend has remained true to the early Sixties ideas of non-violent radical change built out of meaningful, grassroots participatory democracy. Lynd himself sometimes contrasts his political orientation and convictions with those of his celebrated father and mother, Robert and Helen Lynd, best known for writing the groundbreaking Middletown studies of Muncie, Indiana: *Middletown: A Study in Contemporary American Culture* (1929) and *Middletown in Transition* (1937), two enduring classics of American sociology. Robert Lynd was "Old Left" and his son, whom he had such grand ambitions for, Staughton Lynd, was "New Left."

Inspired by Lynd's special libertarian version of New Left activism and thought, I know that an historian can be an agent of radical change in partnership with grassroots radical democracy that empowers the poor as well as despised and oppressed groups. To fully understand and appreciate Lynd's brand of anarchism from the bottom up, and his social democratic ideas, we need context.

As a matter of history, the New Left came out of the termination of Soviet control over the international Marxist-Leninist movement after the astonishing happenings of 1956. Needless to say, these specific events included Nikita Khrushchev's well-known speech denouncing Stalin and his many crimes in addition to the East European revolt of Hungary (and before that Poland) as well as the Soviet reaction. What is more, the resolute opposition made by Maoist and Trotskyist parties around the globe to Soviet ideological management must be considered in any analysis. Later, the Cuban Revolution (1959), the fierce anti-colonial struggles in the Third World, and the Che Guevara legend, suggested to those who clamored for radical change that there were diverse approaches to fundamental political and social transformation, and that other social groups, separate from the modern working class, may well be the instrument of revolutionary change. Undeniably, in Staughton Lynd's non-violent, democratic political universe, it was indeed students, women, racial and ethnic groups, as well as the anti-Vietnam War activists in Europe and the United States, who organized and stood up to challenge the status quo.

Beginning in the Fifties, reaching a highpoint in the Sixties, and even spreading into the Seventies, an assortment of vital social, cultural and political movements struggled to make radical democracy and measurable equality realities in America. A revolutionary notion of democracy enlivened the movements for civil rights and black power, for peace and unity with the Third World, and for gender and sexual equality. Recent scholarship, I believe, interpret the New Left as the broadest-based movement for fundamental change in American history. Like Lynd, they still see the New Left as a work-in-progress in this century in regard to the peace movement, feminism, green parties, and resurgence in thought and action on the Left.

It was American sociologist C. Wright Mills who introduced the term "New Left." He did so in a theoretical document in 1960 titled *Letter to the New Left.* In it he called for a new "leftist" creed to replace the "Old Left" and its emphasis on industrial labor. This new radical paradigm opened up the space for Staughton Lynd and other New Left thinkers and activists. Lynd and other like-minded radicals did not seek to recruit industrial workers, but instead focused on a social activist approach to organization of powerless, marginalized groups.

Staughton Lynd represents the elements of the New Left that were essentially "anarchist" in their orientation. He and others like him looked to libertarian socialist traditions of American radicalism as well as the Industrial Workers of the World (IWW) and shop-floor union militancy. Lynd's brand of New Left activism was also inspired by African American activists such as Bob Moses and the Student Non-violent Coordinating Committee. Lynd's New Left students and organizers, moreover, immersed themselves in poor communities building up grassroots support based on community organizing. Staughton Lynd's New Left sought to be a broad based, grass roots movement.

In any case, nowadays, there is a Staughton Lynd revival taking place in American intellectual life and academic history. Indeed, accolades abound for this renowned historian-activist: "The Admirable Radical" pronounces biographer Carl Mirra; "Legendary Historian, Attorney & Peace Activist," states another source; "Forever Young: Staughton Lynd at 80," proclaims Andy Piascik in a Center for Labor Renewal publication; "The Marching Saint," decrees historian Paul Buhle; "The Return of Staughton Lynd," declares David Waldstreicher in his praise of the recent reprint of the *Intellectual Origins of American Radicalism*.[1]

---

[1]   "For the past fifty years Staughton Lynd has dedicated his life to activism and social change as a historian, lawyer, labor activist and Quaker pacifist. He has been called a saint of the modern American Left," quoted in "Legendary Historian, Attorney & Peace Activist Staughton Lynd on War Resisters, the Peace Movement and the 1993 Lucasville Prison Uprising," http://www.democracynow.org/2006/10/20/legendary_historian_ attorney_peace_activist_staughton; "Suddenly Staughton Lynd is all the rage . . . again. In the last 18 months, Lynd has published two new books, a third that's a reprint of an earlier work, plus a memoir co-authored with his wife Alice," states Andy Piascik in his original essay at the *Connecticut Post*, August 20, 2010 and online at http://www.centerforlaborrenewal. org/.; "Staughton Lynd, although he would never admit it, is one of the visible saints of the modern American left. His life has been full of the determined idealism, small kindnesses and self-abnegation that recall *Catholic Worker* Dorothy Day even better than Socialist Eugene Debs," writes Paul Buhle, May 22, 1997, *The Nation*, (http://www.thenation.com). See also, http://hnn.us/articles/123272.html, for David Waldstreicher's comments.

Lynd is an historian with a place in history. After all, in 1964 he did successfully direct the Freedom Schools in Mississippi during Freedom Summer. Without doubt, however, he will be most remembered for his 1965 trip to Hanoi (North Vietnam) in the company of a young SDS (Students for a Democratic Society) radical Tom Hayden and Communist historian Herbert Aptheker. Now in his eighties and as active as ever, this seemingly ageless Sixties stalwart has moved on from this particular controversy to earn all the tributes noted above. He has merited them through his continuing radical political commitments and boundless energy. In fact, as an independent scholar, Staughton, often in partnership with his accomplished wife Alice (also an attorney and fearless activist), works harder than most full-time academics I know.

Further, the key to understanding the many sides of the protean Staughton Lynd is to recognize his unswerving Heideggerian existential authenticity. Furthermore, Lynd stands out as one of the most important, relevant intellectual-activists in post-World War II America. In the historical profession itself one need only to look at the work of the current generation of colonialists, represented by Duke-trained Woody Holton, Yale-trained David Waldstreicher and many others.[2]

In today's political universe, public intellectuals such as the late Howard Zinn, Noam Chomsky, Sean Wilentz, Tony Judt, and Victor Davis Hanson, among many others, are not unusual. Nonetheless, room must be made for the original, ageless Staughton Lynd, if for no other reason than the depth of his radical thought and the genuineness of his sterling character. In old age, as two truly long distance runners from the Sixties, Staughton and his wife Alice continue to actualize the Herbert Marcuse idea of living in a state of revolutionary ecstasy.

---

[2]   The most recent anthology of essays written by scholars influenced by Lynd-the-historian is *Revolutionary Founders: Rebels, Radicals, and Reformers in the Making of the Nation;* edited by Alfred F. Young, Gary B. Nash, and Ray Raphael. (New York: Alfred A. Knopf, 2011).

Guerrilla History

by Staughton Lynd

Within the past few years we have lost David Montgomery, Alfred Young, and Howard Zinn. Only Jesse Lemisch and I appear to remain from the core group of American historians who in the 1960s began to practice what Jesse called "History from the Bottom Up." I think we need to evaluate what "history from below" has come to mean in practice. I think we need a new working definition of what we intend to do as a community of historians when we write what has been called "the new social history."

"Guerrilla history" is a sub-species or variant of what has been termed "history from below" or "history from the bottom up." But not all history from below is guerrilla history.

In the practice of guerrilla history, the insights of non-academic protagonists are considered to be potentially as valuable as those of the historian. Thus guerrilla history is not a process wherein the poor and oppressed provide poignant facts and a radical academic interprets them. Historical agent and professor of history are understood to be co-workers, together mapping out the terrain traveled and the possibility of openings in the mountain ridges ahead.

A. A Personal Journey

In my own experience, guerrilla history has been a process of discovery, a linked series of moments of enlightenment. I would even speak of "epiphanies."

My wife and I have in our home Webster's Encyclopedic Unabridged Dictionary of the English Language, copyrighted in 1994. It belongs to George Skatzes [pronounced "skates"], sentenced to death as a leader of an 11-day prison uprising in 1993. The prison authorities told George that he could not have such a hard cover book in his cell. But, he was told, if his friends the Lynds divided the book in two, and bound each half in soft covers, the two volumes would be let in. We did as directed but the prison still kept the book out. So for the time being it is our English-language dictionary.

George Skatzes' dictionary defines "epiphany" as "a sudden, intuitive perception of or insight into the reality or essential meaning of something, usually initiated by some simple, homely, or commonplace occurrence or experience."

I think I have experienced four such epiphanies as an historian.

The first was a perception of the American Revolution. As a graduate student, I came to believe that farm tenants and city artisans were primarily concerned with economic survival. Indeed when I later spent several decades among Ohio steelworkers their concerns seemed very similar. Individuals like Tom Paine or, in Youngstown, radical steelworkers Ed Mann and John Barbero, were spectacular exceptions rather than exponents of a generally-shared ideology. There were moments of crisis when Tom Paine or Ed Mann spoke for a class or a community. When the crisis passed each once again found himself to be a marginalized, minority voice.

A second epiphany had to do with the kind of "organizing" undertaken by SNCC and SDS in the 1960s, and the need for what Archbishop Oscar Romero called "accompaniment."

Third, beginning with oral history undertaken in the late 1960s, continuing over a quarter century of close companionship with rank-and-file workers in Youngstown, and reinforced by working-class intellectuals Stan Weir and Marty Glaberman, I have arrived at an idiosyncratic view of the CIO model of trade unionism and a possible better way.

Finally, over the past fifteen years Alice and I have come to know prisoners at the supermaximum security prison near our home. She has acquired the nickname "Mama Bear," and I, "Scrapper."

Let me, with desperate brevity, try to explain.

Farm Tenants and Artisans in the American Revolution

I went to graduate school in the late 1950s to study the American Revolution. The sit-ins and freedom rides had not yet happened. I was anxious to find something good in America on which to build a future. I thought that perhaps I could find it in the years that produced the Declaration of Independence.

Inquiry into the eighteenth century posed the question, How could I do the kind of history in which the informant is considered an equal—the kind of history I came to call "guerrilla history"—with persons who are no longer alive?

I think the answer is that whether the protagonists of interest are dead or alive the historian must listen to them.

Listening to the discontented before and after the American Revolution forced me to discard some preconceptions. Alice and I were living in New York City, trying to survive with two small children on one part-time job and the GI Bill. It seemed natural to study social unrest in the nearby Hudson River valley. It also seemed an attractive subject for someone like myself, seeking to demythologize consensus history and to rescue the reality of class struggle. The Hudson River valley in the 1760s had been the scene of a tenant uprising the leader of which was sentenced to be hanged, drawn, and quartered for treason.

But something peculiar turned up. I held in my hands petitions of tenants in southern Dutchess County asking the revolutionary state legislature to seize the estates of Loyalist landlords and make them available to the tenants who labored on them. So far so good. But only a little further north, near the present site of Bard College, the story was different. There the Continental Congress had strung nets weighted with lead across the Hudson to obstruct the passage of British ships from New York City or Montreal. Nearby tenants had gone out on the river at night, stolen the lead, made bullets with it, and in 1777 rose up . . . in support of George III!

Was this a case of somebody's false consciousness and political confusion? Once one paused to listen the answer was obvious. Whichever side your landlord supported, you chose the other side. In southern Dutchess County the landlords were Loyalists who sheltered Benedict Arnold when he fled across the Hudson. So the tenants became partisans of independence. In northern Dutchess County, however, the owner of Livingston Manor was Robert R. Livingston, a delegate to the Continental Congress and a steadfast, if conservative, patriot. So on Livingston Manor the tenants became Tories. It was not a choice based on ideology. The logic in each case was not false consciousness. It was a rational strategic choice focused on the objective of ownership of the farm on which one labored.

My Master's essay about these goings-on won a prize. My fellow graduate students said, "So now you'll study tenants in other parts of New York." I said, "No, I've got the tenants figured out: I'm curious about urban artisans."

City artisans—shoemakers like that memorably chronicled by Alfred Young, well-to-do metal workers like Paul Revere, laborers in ropewalks like those who became involved in the Boston Massacre—were at the heart of the movement for independence. They were the Sons of Liberty, the folks who specialized in tar and feathers. In the eyes of rich men like Gouverneur Morris the artisans were a dangerous rabble in arms. He famously compared them to rattlesnakes who come out to sun themselves in springtime but can also bite.

Yet after the war, city artisans became enthusiastic supporters of the 1787 Constitution. Charles Beard and Merrill Jensen viewed the movement for the Constitution as a counter-revolutionary coup d'etat. But not only did artisans vote for the new Constitution; in every seacoast city they staged elaborate parades in its support.

What was going on? If, as I did, you read through the newspapers published in New York City during the 1780s, and listened, the answer was once again obvious. Before and after the war for independence, the primary concern of artisans was to keep out of the domestic market imports from the more developed economy in Great Britain. Their situation was like that of Mexican farmers today whose livelihoods have been destroyed by corn and meat imported from Iowa. Hence, before the Revolution, American artisans supported all things anti-British, especially favoring the tactic of non-importation of British goods. And hence, after the Revolution, they supported the Constitution that their class enemy Alexander Hamilton had helped to draft, in hope that it might lead to a strong national tariff sufficient to check the tidal flow of British manufactures into the new United States.

What Happened to SNCC?

In 1961 the Lynds moved to Spelman College in Atlanta. I shared with my colleague Howard Zinn and with students like Alice Walker three years of immersion in the southern civil rights movement. In

1964 I had the honor of coordinating the improvised high schools, the so-called Freedom Schools, of the Mississippi Summer Project.

For those of us who spent the summer of 1964 in Mississippi, the virtual disintegration of the Student Nonviolent Coordinating Committee (SNCC) that Fall was a traumatic sequel. After the mountaintop months of Summer 1964 it was an inexplicable disappointment that so soon afterwards SNCC stumbled and failed to find its way forward.

There were three steps, extending over many years, in my gradual process of understanding what happened.

In June 1967, the day before I was to leave New Haven for Chicago, I ran into Dave Dennis as I was crossing the New Haven Green. Dave had been the principal representative of the Congress of Racial Equality (CORE) in the Summer Project. I invited him to breakfast the next morning.

At breakfast, Dave said that in the winter of 1963-1964 SNCC and CORE staff workers had voted not to invite white volunteers to Mississippi the next summer. Only when news came that Louis Allen, a witness to the murder of Herbert Lee, had himself been murdered, did Dennis and—uncharacteristically—Bob Moses tell CORE and SNCC staff that they must take another vote and reverse their decision. It was one thing for civil rights organizers to risk their lives. It was something else, something unacceptable, that the persons who continued to be killed were longtime local activists like Lee and Allen.

I stored the fact away and began to think about it.

Then, years later, Wesley Hogan, who was working on her book *Many Minds, One Heart,* shared a transcript found in the SNCC archives in Atlanta. The transcript concerned a meeting held in June 1964, just before the summer project began. I had been invited to one session of that meeting since I was to be Freedom Schools coordinator. But it turned out that the evening before there had been a smaller gathering consisting only of SNCC staff.

At that gathering, with hundreds of white volunteers on their way to an orientation program in Ohio and the murders of Chaney, Goodman and Schwerner only a few days in the future, SNCC staff had raised the question: Why are we planning to send delegates of the Mississippi Freedom Democratic Party to the Atlantic City convention of the national Democratic Party with the demand to be seated as delegates? Staff workers Ivanhoe Donaldson and Charlie Cobb, among others, questioned the strategy. The Democratic Party did not seem to them a likely instrument for fundamental social change. Why would one want to become part of it?

This question, unanswered in June, presented itself more traumatically at the Democratic Party convention in August. Anxious not to lose electoral votes in the South, President Lyndon Johnson had refused to consider seating the MFDP delegates, calling Fannie Lou Hamer "that illiterate woman." Hubert Humphrey, Walter Mondale, and Walter Reuther concocted a so-called compromise whereby two MFDP leaders selected by the President would be seated as at-large, non-voting delegates. The civil rights establishment—Roy Wilkins of the NAACP, James Farmer of CORE, Whitney Young of the Urban League, Bayard Rustin, perhaps even Dr. King—urged the MFDP delegates to accept this settlement. They turned it down and returned to Mississippi, disillusioned and disoriented.

Finally, about a year ago, a friend gave me a splendid book about the one substantial project SNCC carried out after Mississippi Summer: *Bloody Lowndes* by Hasan Kwame Jeffries. The book described how Stokely Carmichael and several other SNCC veterans gravitated to Lowndes County, Alabama, because, after the Atlantic City disaster, they wanted to work "outside the Democratic Party." They also wished to pursue with all-black organizers the perspective soon after christened Black Power.

The Lowndes County project got under way in conversations around the edges of the march from Selma to Montgomery in March 1965. "We trailed that march," Stokely recalled. "Every time local folks came out, we'd sit and talk with them, get their names, find out where they lived, their addresses, what church, who their ministers were, like that. So all the information, everything you'd need to organize, we got."

The work went very rapidly and was enormously successful. The Lowndes County Freedom Organization, with its Black Panther logo, came into being. By October 1965 some two thousand African Americans, or 40 percent of the potential black electorate, had become registered voters. In the county election of November 1966, black candidates trailed white candidates by a few hundred votes, but in a locality where African Americans were the majority, eventual electoral success seemed assured.

However, shortly after the 1966 election, although SNCC had been in Lowndes County less than two years, the organization withdrew its staff. Why did this happen?

The answer is that SNCC was following the prevailing organizing doctrine of the 1960s, practiced by labor unions, by community organizers instructed by Saul Alinsky, and by both black and white students. Chuck McDew, one of SNCC's first chairpersons, put it this way.

> [M]any SNCC staffers had always viewed the committee as a short-lived group of organizers who would eventually organize themselves out of a job. We said that if we go more than five years or if we go without an understanding or feeling that the organization would be disbanded, we will run the risk of becoming institutionalized and spending more time trying to perpetuate the institution than having the freedom to act and do.

Stokely Carmichael offered precisely the same reason for leaving Lowndes County after staying there so briefly.

> Our way is to live in the community, find, train, or develop representative leadership within strong, accountable local organizations or coalitions that did not exist before, and that are capable of carrying on the struggle after we leave. When we succeed in this, we will work ourselves out of a job. Which is our goal.

Accordingly, if one asks, Why didn't SNCC develop a long-range strategy for making use of the vote to challenge the poverty and economic oppression of African Americans, it seems that most SNCC organizers did not believe in long-range strategies. Even before the Summer Project, I tried to raise the question several times, asking, "Doesn't the Movement need a strategy like the demand for forty acres and a mule after the Civil War?" The response that I got was, "You want us to have an ideology."

In Lowndes County, SNCC's withdrawal did not work out as Stokely Carmichael had hoped. After another electoral defeat by about the same margin as in 1966, the leaders of the Lowndes County Freedom Organization decided to drop the Black Panther logo. They successfully advocated at a mass meeting that the local party should merge with a statewide African American party that supported the Democratic Party's national candidates. And John Hulett, longtime leader of the Lowndes County movement, began to cut deals with his white counterparts without authorization from the party's rank and file. Not long after the 1972 election Hulett decided to join the Democratic Party.

Youthful organizers associated with Students for a Democratic Society (SDS) experienced a similar cycle of short-term successes and longer-term disappointment. Like Stokely Carmichael in Lowndes County, white students who dropped out of school, moved to an inner city, and sought to organize "an interracial movement of the poor," did not stay very long. In fact Northern Student Movement organizer Peter Countryman at one point wrote to SNCC staff member Tim Jenkins that there was needed a group of people who would "for two months live in one room apartments and eat hamburgers and . . . go into the community, and talk the language of the people and be sensitive to their problems."

Two months? Even two years? This was the monumental fallacy of believing that one could enter a new situation in which one was a total stranger, very likely live together with other self-styled "organizers" in a Freedom House unlike anything ever before experienced in the neighborhood, offer local residents no discernible expertise such as a teacher, a doctor, or a lawyer might provide, leave after two months or two years, and expect to bring about revolutionary social change.

SDS activists in the inner cities of the North, like the great majority of their counterparts in the Mississippi Delta or Lowndes County, failed to stay in the communities where they were organizing for more than two or three years. Jennifer Frost concludes her definitive study of the SDS Economic Research and Action Project (ERAP) with these words:

> [N]ot enough New Left organizers understood or appreciated community organizing . . . as the slow, undramatic, and long-term process of helping people develop their powers . . . . New Left participants failed to adopt a model for lifelong organizing. Most followed

> SNCC's example of young people "dropping out" from schools or careers for a few years of full-time organizing . . . . ERAP failed to develop a model of organizing . . . they could sustain over the long haul. Instead their approach led to exhaustion and "burnout."

Eric Mann, an ERAP volunteer in Newark, belatedly came to the insight that what was needed was the "long-distance runner thing."

Accompaniment

There is another model. It originated in Latin America and calls itself "accompaniment." Its fullest exemplification was in the life and writing of Archbishop Oscar Romero of El Salvador in the years just before Romero's assassination.

Vatican II and the pronouncements of Latin American bishops at their gatherings in Medellin, Colombia (1968) and Puebla, Mexico (1979) popularized the concept of a "preferential option for the poor." Adding to and deepening this concept in his Fourth and last Pastoral Letter, Monsignor Romero called for what he termed "an apostolate of following or companionship."

This idea of accompaniment was embodied in the "despedida" or dismissal that ends the Salvadoran campesino mass. The popular mass was created during the last years of Monsignor Romero's life as a group product of the priests with whom he worked and the peasants who made up their congregations. "When the poor come to believe in the poor," the mass affirms, "yes, then we will be able to sing of liberty." One finds a similar idea in the words that sum up the Zapatista vision: to lead by obeying ("mandar obediciendo") in quest of another world ("un otro mundo").

To offer a snapshot, it is what Alice and I experienced during a week in 1990 that we spent with Sisters Nellie and Carmencita of the Little Sisters of Jesus in the almost unimaginably poor hamlet of El Bonete in northwest Nicaragua. Alice was enlisted to get the two village sewing machines running again, and, contrary to all rational predictions, was able to do it. There followed adventures in making trousers for a child from one leg of a woman's pair of pants and searching the entire settlement for a button. I was considerably less useful as a digger of ditches intended to make available piped water in place of two ancient wells. It was too hot to do any kind of work at midday and so one dozed under a shelf that held the Sisters' library: writings of Romero and Che Guevara, and three copies of a handbook for communities without a physician, *Where There Is No Doctor*. Once each day we spent time with the Sisters in a tiny chapel adjacent to their home. The altar was a tree stump. We sat on cinder blocks or floor mats. They taught us songs in Spanish and we sang American civil rights songs. On one wall Carmencita, who was from El Salvador, had embroidered Romero's words: Unless a grain falls into the earth and dies, there can be no new life. I felt that I had finally found in the lives of these two women the preferential option for the poor.

SNCC and SDS organizers no doubt believed that they were opting for the poor and practicing accompaniment when they devoted their lives, and in the South, risked their lives, to work among the marginalized and oppressed for a few years. Romero envisioned a longer-term commitment.

What About the Workers?

When Alice and I moved to Chicago in 1967 the student movement was turning toward a strategy of imagined working-class revolution. Working-class young men were being drafted to fight in Vietnam and beginning to resist the orders of their officers. As in the 1930s, a significant number of middle-class young people were leaving the campus to become steelworkers or workers in automobile plants.

Alice and I sought to evaluate the world of working-class experience by doing oral histories. "Go see so-and-so," we would be told, and led in this way from one person to the next we put together the book *Rank and File*. We created occasions when veterans of the labor movement who had become organizers in the 1930s could share what they had learned with the new generation of would-be-radicals. We helped to convene a Writers' Workshop in Gary where a variety of persons told their stories.

I had the opportunity to meet steelworker John Sargent. He had been president of the Steel Workers Organizing Committee at Inland Steel in East Chicago, Indiana in the 1930s. Later, when the CIO was recognized as exclusive bargaining representative, he became president of the 18,000-member local union of the United Steelworkers of America at Inland. He was re-elected in 1943, 1944, 1946, and, despite vicious Red-baiting, 1964. When we met him he was again working as an electrician in the mill.

In March 1970, John shared his story at a forum held in a community college in northwest Indiana on the topic, "Labor History from the Standpoint of the Rank and File." John told those in attendance that the Little Steel strike of 1937, which most labor historians consider a catastrophic defeat, was a "victory of great proportions." None of the striking unions won a contract, he explained. What they got was an agreement through the governor's office that the company would recognize and bargain with "the Steelworkers Union and the company union and any other organization that wanted to represent the people in the steel industry."

The arrangement was what Professor Charles Morris has recently written a book about, calling it "minority" or "members-only" unionism. John Sargent described it as follows:

> Without a contract, without any agreement with the company, without any regulations concerning hours of work, conditions of work, or wages, a tremendous surge took place. We talk of a rank-and-file movement; the beginning of union organization was the best kind of rank-and-file movement you could think of . . . . The union organizers were essentially workers in the mill who were so disgusted with their conditions and so ready for a change that they took the union into their own hands.

Without a contract, John continued,

> we secured for ourselves agreements on working conditions and wages that we do not have today [1970]. For example, as a result of the enthusiasm of the people in the mill you had a series of strikes, wildcats, shut-downs, slow-downs, anything working people could think of to secure for themselves what they decided they had to have. If their wages were low there was no contract to prohibit them from striking, and they struck for better wages. If their conditions were bad, if they didn't like what was going on, if they were being abused,

the people in the mills themselves—without a contract or any agreement with the company involved—would shut down a department or even a group of departments to secure for themselves the things they found necessary.

Sargent went on to say that in the late 1930s, steelworkers at Inland came to an understanding with the company pursuant to which Inland Steel agreed to pay no less than its competitors for a given kind of work. All that a union representative had to do was to prove to the company that a particular category of workers, for example on the pickle line, were being paid less than their counterparts at, say, Youngstown Sheet & Tube. And if that was a fact, steelworkers on the pickle line at Inland Steel were given a wage increase.

Nick Migas, grievance committee person in the crucial open hearth department, tells in his own narrative in *Rank and File* how things were done during the Sargent era. Every month, union members in each department would meet at the union hall, discuss their immediate problems, and decide what to do about them. In later years, a man would file a grievance, a steward would take it up, and the aggrieved worker might never hear of it again. But in those early days, Migas said, "the man who had the grievance came right along with me . . . . He went with me to the next step . . . . He was always there."

Migas recalled an incident when the company wouldn't resolve a complaint from the charging car operators. "So that night it started to slow down, and by the next morning there were two furnaces where they had to shut the heat off. They settled the grievance in a hurry. Nobody told anybody to strike. There was just that close relationship, working with the people, where they knew what was necessary."

Clearly what John Sargent and Nick Migas felt that they had learned at Inland Steel in the 1930s was very similar to the analysis projected a generation earlier by the Industrial Workers of the World (IWW). A comprehensive collective bargaining agreement, assumed by today's labor historians and union organizers to be self-evidently desirable, and which I too took for granted before talking to John Sargent and colleagues, was for these men often an obstacle. At Inland Steel, local union officers were empowered by the 1937 strike settlement that obligated management to bargain with their members-only union. They felt that they were in a stronger position before the union was recognized as exclusive bargaining representative than they were afterwards. Today's typical contract clauses prohibiting strikes during the life of the agreement, and giving the company the sole right to make investment decisions like shutting down a plant, did not yet exist. The local union could decide for itself what actions it wished to take in response to particular problems as they arose.

This is a perspective almost unimaginably heretical from the standpoint of today's union leaders and their academic supporters. I entitled the article in which I first reported the experience of John Sargent, "Guerrilla History in Gary." It appeared in *Liberation* magazine and has been re-printed in a collection of my fugitive writings, *From Here to There*.

The hypothesis that emerged from my encounter with John Sargent might be stated as follows. It has been suggested that the CIO took a wrong path as a result of Supreme Court cases (Karl Klare), or because of a culture of arbitration that developed during World War II when CIO unions agreed not to strike (James Atleson), or because of the Taft-Hartley Act and CIO purges (David Montgomery and others). I believe the problem was the pattern of collective bargaining imposed on the new CIO unions at their very beginnings by John L. Lewis, a dictator within his own union. The critical elements of that pattern were:

>A single union as exclusive bargaining representative;
>
>The dues check-off, whereby the employer became dues collector for the union and the union became less accountable to its members;
>
>The management prerogatives clause, which authorized the company to make all the big investment decisions, including closing a plant;
>
>Above all, a no-strike clause that prevented workers from doing anything about those decisions.

The Worst of the Worst

Alice and I retired from Legal Services in 1996 and for almost twenty years have advocated for prisoners as *pro bono* counsel for the American Civil Liberties Union of Ohio.

All steelmaking in Youngstown, once the second or third largest steel-producing city in the country, had been shut down. It is my unproven hypothesis that Youngstown's City Fathers deliberately decided to substitute prisons for steel mills. What is a fact is that the Mayor of Youngstown described the State's decision to locate Ohio's supermaximum security prison in our community as a "home run." Within half an hour's drive from our home there are now the supermax, Ohio's first private prison, a major "close security" prison, as well as a reconstructed city jail. A new federal prison, where Father Phil Berrigan was confined toward the end of his life, is only a little further away.

Since Alice has taken the lead in our prison advocacy, I like to introduce myself as her driver. And I am going to let her tell about this phase of our experience as guerrilla historians in paragraphs quoted from our joint memoir, *Stepping Stones*.

> When Lessley [Harmon, whom we had come to know in a group called Workers Against Toxic Chemical Hazards, or WATCH], was imprisoned only a half hour drive from where we live, Lessley asked us to do the paperwork necessary to be placed on his visiting list. For six years, until Lessley was transferred to a distant prison, we visited Lessley nearly every month. Every visit led us to new questions and new insights.
>
> . . . [W]hen Ohio decided to build a supermaximum security prison in Youngstown, we were contacted by staff of the American Friends Service Committee telling us someone was needed to monitor what went on inside that facility. Furthermore, a national campaign against control units was planned for April 1996 and we were asked to plan an event in Youngstown.
>
> We knew nothing about "supermax prisons" or "control units" where prisoners are kept in solitary confinement for twenty-three or twenty-four hours a day for years, and where physical and mental abuse is sometimes rampant. I began by reading all the articles I could obtain on conditions in supermaximum security prisons and the psychological effects of prolonged solitary confinement, not only on the prisoners but also on the guards in such prisons.

. . . I drafted a paper called "What Is A Supermax Prison" and I invited people on the mailing lists of the Workers' Solidarity Club of Youngstown and the Youngstown Peace Council to a meeting. Fifteen people came. I read my paper and then asked, "Does anyone want to do something about this?" "Yes." "What?" "Plan an educational forum."

A woman who lived near the site arranged for us to hold the first forum on land within sight of the cranes that were building what was later named the Ohio State Penitentiary (OSP) . . . . Nearly a hundred people came.

I wanted one of the speakers at the forum to be a person who had been held in prolonged solitary confinement, or a close relative of such a person. I found both. One of them was Jackie Bowers, sister of George Skatzes . . . who had recently been sentenced to death for his alleged role as a leader of the prison uprising at Lucasville, Ohio in April 1993 . . . .

Jackie put us in touch with the lawyer who would handle George's appeal. The lawyer told us that someone needed to read the entire record and then look for information that should have been in the trial record but was not. We first visited George in the fall of 1996 and [until Staughton's bypass operation in June 2008] tried to visit him every month.

George introduced us to other prisoners sentenced to death for their supposed roles in the Lucasville disturbance, Jason Robb and Keith LaMar. Jason and Siddique Abdullah Hasan, a Muslim imam alleged by the State to be the principal leader of the uprising, lent us papers from their trials. We began to correspond with them as well . . . .

In early May 1998, we received letters from Jason and Hasan. They said that they had been awakened one morning at four o'clock and told to pack their personal property, they were going to Youngstown. They were among the first prisoners to arrive at OSP . . .

A week later, George Skatzes was sent to Youngstown. Staughton and I made the first visit by anyone to any prisoner at OSP. George was in a booth where he sat for two hours on a fixed stool with his feet chained and his hands cuffed behind his back. A glass partition separated him from the booth in which we were locked. A correctional officer sat just outside George's side of the booth.

. . . Early in 1999, a prisoner newly transferred to OSP committed suicide. In July 1999, I received letters telling me that another prisoner was suicidal, had been released from suicide watch and was being taunted by guards. I sent an inquiry to the Warden's assistant. A week later we got a phone call from the Warden's assistant telling us, "He's dead." The Warden's assistant asked us what we thought OSP could do to give the prisoners more of a sense that life was worth living. Staughton and I responded for about an hour.

After the phone call, I said to Staughton, 'They should ask the prisoners rather than us." I drafted a form that said, "If someone asked you, WHAT COULD OSP DO TO MAKE YOU FEEL YOUR LIFE IS MORE WORTH LIVING, what would you say?" I wrote a covering letter in which I said, You don't have to respond if you don't want to, you don't have to sign your name if you do respond, but say only what it is OK for me to submit to the administration. I sent the form and the letter to 100 prisoners at OSP. Not everyone responded, but I received 110 responses!

These responses led to a class action law suit in which several of the men who responded to Alice's letter became witnesses concerning various aspects of their confinement. What was fact-finding for an eventual lawsuit was, at the same time, fact-finding for a history of supermax confinement in Youngstown. I like to say that the only difference between being a historian and being a lawyer is that, as a lawyer, after you come up with the facts of an unjust situation there is a dessert: you are allowed to try to do something about it.

A personal epiphany for me was to question thirteen of these men, in the eyes of the State of Ohio among the so-called "worst of the worst," one after the other in federal court. Alice had selected the witnesses and prepared their papers to be used as exhibits. Their testimony won the case for us and established a minimum of due process, now required by the United States Supreme Court before a prisoner can be placed in supermax confinement anywhere in the United States.

The "Lucasville Five"—the five men condemned to death after the 1993 uprising at the Southern Ohio Correctional Facility—not only provided evidence concerning their confinement at OSP but deep insight into what George Skatzes calls the "criminal injustice system." Through them we learned of the doctrine of the "death-qualified" jury, which excludes from a jury in a capital case all persons categorically opposed to the death penalty, while permitting equally strong advocates of the death penalty to serve, provided they promise to follow the judge's legal instructions. Likewise the Five emphasized the fact that there was very little physical evidence or objective evidence of any kind to support their convictions. They were sentenced to death almost wholly on the basis of testimony from other prisoners who received benefits in exchange for their testimony, such as no indictment, dropped charges, new sentences that ran concurrently rather than consecutively with time to which they were already sentenced, or a letter to the parole board.

Finally, speaking of epiphanies, Alice and I must witness to the relationship of trust that has become possible with the Five. The one who is closest to execution recently wrote to me:

> I'm doing all right, my friend. Thank you for "accompanying" me on this rough and difficult (scary) path. I can't begin to tell you how much I appreciate it. And thank you for being my friend, Scrapper. It truly is an honor to have access to you and Alice. I often tell the story of this man who set out to circumnavigate the globe in a one-man boat. Halfway through, the boat capsized and the man had to abort the trip. A few months later, while doing an interview, he was asked "how does it feel to fail?" And he answered, "I didn't fail. I saw things that people will never see: eighty foot waves, whales, beautiful sunsets." In a very real sense, this is how I feel. I would have never met you and Alice had I decided to cop out; and to that you may say, "Well, I don't think meeting us was worth the trouble." I don't agree. People live their whole life without ever having a true friend, without ever knowing what it feels like to stand

up and speak truth to power. And, yes, I may lose in the end; but even if my worst fears come true, I will still be able to say, "I've lived . . . and I know how it feels to really love somebody." So it's worth it, my friend. Even if I lose, I will never feel that I've failed. I'm living my life to the fullest!

B. Practicing Guerrilla History

Connecting History from the Bottom Up with the "Master Narrative" of the Nation or the World

Typically, history from below has taken the form of portraying the experience of this or that group of poor and oppressed people at a particular point in the past. Exactly how what we have found challenges mainstream accounts is often not addressed. As a result, Tom Humphrey has commented, we "have heretofore only succeeded in pressing the authors of the master narrative, which largely ignores class and class struggle, to alter their stories slightly or, worse, to add another box for 'the poor' on the margins" of the page. The Establishment has been willing to give us the stories of chimney sweeps who get cancer, or seamstresses who burn to death when the foreman locks the door, provided we leave undisturbed the belief that the United States is an exceptionally admirable place, the history of which other societies should do their best to imitate.

Speaking of foremen, there has recently been published an exciting example of history from below by Henry Wiencek. Wiencek wrote an earlier book in which he told how President George Washington directed an employee of the United States Customs Service to kidnap and return to servitude a house slave of Mrs. Washington who had run away. His new book is about Jefferson.

According to Wiencek's new book, *Master of the Mountain*, the previous editor of Jefferson's Farm Book withheld important details about the nailworks that Jefferson launched in 1794 as the unprofitability of tobacco became manifest. Two months of production in the nailworks paid the entire annual grocery bill for Jefferson's household. African American boys ten to sixteen years old worked in the nailery until they were able to do field work. The boys were whipped when they were late to work.

But in 1798 the foreman, a black man named Great George Granger, seems to have refused to whip the juvenile workers. Jefferson's son-in-law Thomas Mann Randolph apparently took charge of discipline. When one of the child laborers hit another with a hammer, Jefferson himself ordered that the assailant be sold away "so distant as never more to be heard of among us."

Wiencek's new book on Jefferson does not back away from confronting the presumed celebrity of those whom Jesse Lemisch called Great White Men. It describes the world of Monticello when "seen from below" as a world in which "the bottom subsidized the top."

History of "the People"

The political atmosphere of the American Left in the late 1930s was permeated by a "Popular Front" strategy adopted by the international Communist movement in 1935. Concerned to bring together all so-called progressive forces that might oppose German expansion and an attack on the Soviet Union, Communists, by far the most numerous variety of radicals, sought to coalesce with persons and groups whom they had denounced during the so-called "Third Period," 1929-1935. The concept of "the people," as in Carl Sandburg's poem "The People, Yes," replaced an emphasis on class. The supposed existence of a democratic tradition represented by Jefferson, Jackson (!), and Lincoln was affirmed. Communism was described as twentieth-century Americanism. I remember well the hootenannys and Spanish Civil War songs of my youth, as well as Pete Seeger's appearance at annual gatherings of *The National Guardian* a quarter century later.

David Montgomery, Al Young, and Howard Zinn came to adulthood in this atmosphere before I did. With each of them, I came to a moment when, as it seemed to me, my colleagues sought to find a positive, unified spirit in a popular movement when I found a more prosaic scattering of sentiments, and sometimes demoralizing compromise and conflict.

As an editorial consultant for the University of Illinois Press, David disapproved of my introduction to a book of essays on the "alternative trade unionism" of the early 1930s. I believe he thought that the CIO was doing fine until its encounter with McCarthyism after World War II.

Al Young and I experienced a similar moment of mutual incomprehension concerning the artisan parades in major seacoast cities that celebrated the new Constitution of 1787. He saw in the floats and banners of these parades an efflorescence of popular culture. I asked in vain, but what about the fact that the artisans, the shock troops of the independence struggle, threw their support to a plan of government drafted by traditional class enemies?

The last scholarly production that Al helped to create was a book of essays entitled *Revolutionary Founders*. The leading conclusion of the book is that "Common farmers, artisans, and laborers often led the resistance to imperial policies." My own doctoral research suggested that the most exploited and vulnerable groups in the mainland British colonies typically lived through the independence struggle in a localized, pragmatic manner, some supporting the patriot cause but others opposing it. African American slaves and Native Americans made a variety of inconsistent choices, weighing imagined opportunities against dreaded consequences. I was unable to pursue these insights with Al Young.

Finally, Howard and I were unable to discuss, as historians, the disintegration of the Student Nonviolent Coordinating Committee (SNCC) after the 1964 national Democratic Party convention.

But here I want to offer an amendment to my general thesis about the influence of Popular Front politics on the work of the first generation of American historians who practiced history from the bottom up.

I believe Howard Zinn may be more remembered for his anti-war advocacy than for his *People's History*. He was a World War II bombardier who came to feel that no conceivable modern war could be just. As he eventually viewed the matter, it was inevitable that any modern war would involve dropping bombs on civilians and, especially, children, from a height or distance such that the bombardier cannot see, or hear, or smell, the consequences. As Yossarian concluded in *Catch-22*, one of Howard's favorite books when I knew him in Atlanta, "the enemy" might include one's own commanding officers.

Howard's last public address was delivered on November 11, the date that used to be called "Armistice Day." The text of this speech is available in a collection entitled *Howard Zinn Speaks*, edited by Anthony Arnove. The speech is entitled "Three Holy Wars." Of course Howard meant, unholy wars. The three unholy wars were the American Revolution, the Civil War, and World War II.

In this address Howard criticized what are generally viewed—by historians, including many Left historians, and by the general public—as the three great people's triumphs of our national history. How, Howard asked, can one criticize events that brought about independence, an end to slavery, and the defeat of fascism? He proceeded to do so.

Slaves didn't benefit from the American Revolution, he argued. Likewise Native Americans lost ground—literally as well as figuratively—because there was no longer a British proclamation attempting to halt the westward movement of settlement at the crest of the Appalachians.

Was there a way to become independent without a war? Canada did it. It took Canada longer than the United States to become independent, but, Howard commented, "[s]ometimes it takes longer if you don't want to kill."

Similarly Howard asked about the Civil War if the same result might have been achieved without the deaths of hundreds of thousands of combatants. (After Howard's death, new research using census records placed the number of deaths of Union and Confederate soldiers at three quarters of a million.) There is no way to be sure, he conceded. But, he remarked, "slavery was ended in every other country in the Western Hemisphere [Haiti excepted]" without "a bloody civil war." Howard finished with what became a characteristic theme at the end of his life, as it is of mine: "When soldiers refuse to fight . . . wars can't go on."

The History of Our Own Movement

Nobody wants to tell other historians what they should study and write about. But surely we who describe our point of view as—quoting Subcomandante Marcos—"below and to the Left," have some responsibility to grapple with the history of our own Movement.

I have found some strange notions among the young people in Occupy as to why SNCC, SDS and the Black Panthers crashed and burned at the end of the 1960s. One Occupier told me that it was all the fault of COINTELPRO.

I disagree. No matter how infiltrated and provoked, we ourselves were principally responsible for the disintegration of our beloved organizations.

I remember a large public meeting in Chicago where a member of the SDS national executive committee spoke of "icing" and "offing"—that is, killing—persons with whom one disagreed politically. When Mumia published an otherwise excellent book on the Black Panthers, he derided the prosecutors in the New Haven trial who claimed that the Panthers killed one of their own members. I sent him the *New York Times* obituary of the man who later confessed to having done exactly that. Mumia said he would correct what he had said in a revised edition, yet to appear.

Moreover, I think we need to ask ourselves, What historical perspective have we bequeathed to our younger colleagues? Marxism and liberalism share a hopeful vision of the future. Whether one speaks the language of the Hegelian waltz—thesis, antithesis, synthesis; one, two, three; one, two, three—or, simply, of Progress, the two ideologies converge on an expectation that things will get better. But the events of the last century—fascism, the Moscow purge trials, the holocaust, Hiroshima and Nagasaki, the collapse of the Soviet Union, and the disappointing evolution of Polish Solidarity and Israeli Zionism—call that expectation into question.

I think we should ask our comrades in Occupy to speak for themselves, but if I might anticipate, I think their sense of the matter goes something like this: Things are not getting better. Indeed, in recent years the prospect of global warming has been added to the failures of the past century. The truth (this is still Occupy talking) is that humanity has been in bad shape ever since the period of hunting and gathering. Once you had settled agriculture, and a predictable annual surplus, you got central bureaucracies, taxes, and armies. The strategy of taking over the state, whether by radicals or liberals, only perpetuates such oppression in new forms. From time to time there will be widespread popular upsurges, as in the United States in the 1930s or in Chiapas today, that may reignite hope but tend to be temporary. For the moment, we can only create exilic spaces, refuges on the margins.

This take on history resembles that of Frances Fox Piven and Richard Cloward in their book *Poor People's Movements*. They argued that history does not move forward through step-by-step realization of progressive ideas, as liberals might suggest, or because of the leadership of radical organizations, the view favored on the Left. Rather, in agreement with anarchists and Occupiers, Piven and Cloward find that change for the better takes the form of historical lunges prompted by uproar in the streets, which lose their impact when institutionalized.

Such differences exist beneath the surface of daily activity, are difficult to discern and articulate, and awkward to resolve. Nevertheless, I think that it might help to forestall future defeats if we could come to reasoned consensus about why and how the Movement of the 1960s came to an end.

Can One Be Both a Good Historian and a Radical Activist?

When I became a graduate student of history, Alice prophesied that I would find the practice of academic history two-dimensional and unsatisfying. She was right. But when my activity against the Vietnam war caused me to be thrust out of the Ivy League, it made possible entry into the worlds of draft resisters, steelworkers, Palestinians, and prisoners, that I would not otherwise have experienced. "Guerrilla history" with these new friends provided a third dimension that history put together solely from old documents found in cold buildings could not.

Meantime Alice had been doing anti-war work of her own as a draft counselor. She developed the idea that when counselor and counselee encounter one another, there is a meeting of "two experts." One is an expert on Selective Service regulations, and on the customary practice of draft boards. The other is an expert on his own life: what he carried into adulthood from church attendance as a child and adolescent; his expectations and those of his parents and wife or girl friend; his imagined ability to deal with the rigors of foreseeable incarceration; what he wishes to have become by middle age.

This became our model for how we, as paralegals and attorneys, should relate to our clients. And it became the model as well for how I should function as a "guerrilla historian" away from academia.

I had the opportunity to discuss this question with Edward Thompson. He answered the question explicitly, telling me: Yes, one can do good history and engage in productive activism, but one cannot do both at the same time.

Edward Thompson laid down his life prematurely in the years he devoted to opposing nuclear weapons in Europe. But it also seems pertinent that Thompson wrote his greatest work of history, *The Making of the English Working Class*, while serving, outside academia, as an itinerant lecturer for a workers' education program in the north of England. This fact is consistent with my belief that the protagonist in a movement may become its best historian. I myself found that exile from the academy enriched my work as an historian. Because I had been blacklisted and forced out of academia against my will I was able to reinvent myself as a lawyer, and thus disguised, immerse myself in the experience of rank-and-file steelworkers and high-security prisoners.

I learned that many people who do manual work for a living or wake up within prison walls are indeed caught up in the necessities of survival. Rather than basing their conduct on ideology, they feel obliged to look first to self-interest.

But I also learned that ordinary people often exhibit solidarity, at least within the circle of those in daily contact with each other, and sometimes, prophetic vision as well. In a book of rank-and-file narratives, Alice and I presented the account of a union organizer named Mia Giunta [pronounced "junta"]. Mia had helped poor and immigrant workers at a Connecticut factory to organize a local union of the United Electrical Workers. The CIO's signature achievement is thought to have been the seniority system. But helpful as such contract language may be in hiring and promotions, a mechanical application of seniority during a layoff tends to destroy solidarity and victimize the most recent hires, often minorities or women. So at the F-Dyne factory, as Mia Giunta told its story, it became customary to negotiate separate layoff agreements pursuant to which all employees, regardless of date of hire, shared the available work equally. According to an article by David Montgomery and Ronald Schatz in the magazine *Radical America*, work-sharing of this sort was common before the 1930s. Something very similar occurred in the 1980s among a group of visiting nurses whom my wife and I helped to organize a union. Indeed, in our own Legal Services office, when President Ronald Reagan cut the national Legal Services budget by 20 percent, all the lawyers in the Youngstown office "went down" to four days of work a week. In these varied situations, workers spontaneously helped to create what the late Stan Weir called a "family at work."

Perhaps radicalism can be defined as the nurturing and, especially, helping to broaden, such circles of solidarity. And perhaps the historian has an exciting and challenging role to play in that essential work.

Personally, in the short run I keep trying to understand what happened in the Lucasville, Ohio prison uprising of 1993, and the resistance currently underway in high security prisons in California.

My project for the medium run is to learn more about the early history of the Zapatistas. The Zapatistas seem to me the most hopeful phenomenon on earth at the present moment. And I have two questions about their very early history. How was it that a small group of Marxists were able to transplant themselves from Mexico City to the Lacondón jungle, live there amid the rain and spiders for ten years, and emerge on January 1, 1994 as part of a revolutionary insurgency? And second, as John Womack has shown, the Declaration that the Zapatistas issued when they went public on that day was a traditional Leninist summons to march on the national capitol, win over the soldiers of the government's army, and take state power. Within a matter of weeks they had changed their minds, and proclaimed that they would leave the democratization of Mexico to others and dig in where they lived, in Chiapas.

Why did these things happen? How did they happen? What is their history?

C. Conclusion

What is the "more" that must be lovingly nurtured, must come into being more fully, must pervade the good society, the "otro mundo," of our dreams? It is precisely that which the practice of guerrilla history seeks to enhance: the awakening, ultimately the self-awakening, of ordinary people. In accompanying the poor and oppressed, one seeks to promote the epiphanies of self-awakening. It is this that a professional can contribute to the struggle for fundamental change. This is the experience to which academics trained to protect themselves, to insulate their research and their lives, need to be open. The working-class poet D.H. Lawrence said it this way:

What is the knocking?
What is the knocking at the door in the night?
It is somebody come to do us harm.
No, no, it is the three strange angels.
Admit them, admit them.

Howard Zinn

by Staughton Lynd

Presented on April 9, 2010 at the Organization of American Historians session called Remembering Howard Zinn, hosted by the The Labor and Working-Class History Association (LAWCHA) and Historians Against the War (HAW).

It may seem a strange form of grieving: To remember a friend, who happens to have been an historian, by seeking to discern what kind of historian he was, what vision of history he sought to present, what in the way of history we might wish to carry forward from what he accomplished. Nonetheless that is the project in which I invite you to join me.

A good place to begin an assessment of Howard Zinn as an historian is where he himself began: his Master's essay on the Ludlow Massacre of 1914.(1) Howard had been about fourteen years old in 1937, the year of the sit-down strike in Flint, Michigan and the Republic Steel Massacre. Later he worked for three years as an apprentice steamfitter. He read "books about fascism in Europe" and admired Communist friends who were "ferociously antifascist."(2) It should come as no surprise that this self-taught working-class intellectual chose as his first academic subject what he called "perhaps the most violent struggle between corporate power and laboring men in American history." Ludlow, he added, remains "an obscure event, rarely mentioned in textbooks on American history" such as the *Encyclopedia of American History*, edited by Richard Morris, or Samuel Eliot Morison's *Oxford History of the American People*. (3)

In the aftermath of Howard's death some question has been raised as to whether he was really an historian, and more particularly, whether he was able to produce the paradigmatic product of the academic historian: detailed narrative history based on fully-cited primary sources. His account of the Ludlow Massacre should put that question to rest. It is available in Howard's book, *The Politics of History*.

But the detailed rendering of a particular event did not satisfy Howard. He makes this crystal clear at the end of his Ludlow essay, where he writes:

> How shall we read the story of the Ludlow massacre? As another "interesting" event of the past? Or as supporting evidence for an analysis of that long present which spans 1914 and 1970 [the year in which he was writing]. If it is read narrowly, as an incident in the history of the trade union movement and the coal industry, then it is an angry splotch in the past, fading rapidly amidst new events. If it is read as a commentary on a larger question—the relationship of government to corporate power and of both to movements of social protest—then we are dealing with the present. (4)

Howard's work on the Southern civil rights movement followed Howard's years of apprenticeship at Columbia. Howard and his family moved to Atlanta when he was offered a job there. He taught at Spelman College from 1956 to 1963. Following his abrupt and unjust dismissal in June 1963, he used the year's salary that came with the discharge letter to write two books: *The Southern Mystique* and *SNCC: The New Abolitionists*.

In the book on the Student Nonviolent Coordinating Committee, or SNCC, Howard's account of the movement in Albany, Georgia is as taut and detailed as his essay on Ludlow. The difference is that in his writing about SNCC there are fewer footnotes. Howard drew on personal experience and oral history as well as written sources. His mini-histories of Albany, McComb, Hattiesburg, and the Mississippi Delta remain the building blocks for the subsequent work of scholars such as Clayborne Carson, Charles Payne and Wesley Hogan.

The Southern Mystique is in some ways a more interesting book than its better-known counterpart. Recall that in connection with the Ludlow essay Howard asserts that historians must "remove enough of the historical detail" from their accounts "so that common ground can be found . . . between another period and our own." (5) In effect, history must be reported in a way that makes possible sociological generalization.

Living in Atlanta through the years of sit-ins and Freedom Rides, Howard took a further step, formulating a methodology that would inform everything he later wrote. Everyone we knew struggled with the question: What was the best way to end racial segregation? Should it be sought by small, incremental steps that would gradually change attitudes? Or should there be decreed from above across-the-board change in the institutional environment, to which, in the course of time, whites would adjust first their conduct, and then their thinking?

Howard came down emphatically in favor of the second strategy. The example that seemed most compelling was the racial integration of the Armed Forces, which was only indirectly a product of history from below but most obviously was caused by orders from President Truman. A dozen years later it appeared to be working.

The Southern Mystique articulates a sophisticated rationale for this top down strategy. Persons inclined to dismiss Howard Zinn as a shallow popularizer should take a look at the "Bibliographical Notes" to this book. Here one finds works of history, like Stanley Elkins' *Slavery*, *The Strange Career of Jim Crow*, W. E. B. DuBois' *The Souls of Black Folk*, From Slavery to Freedom by John Hope Franklin, and *The Mind of the South*; of sociology, by Ross, Cooley, Mannheim, Merton, and Franklin Frazier; of social psychology, by Harry Stack Sullivan, Kurt Lewin, and Gardner Murphy; as well as classics of the day by Herbert Marcuse and Norman Brown.

The argument of *The Southern Mystique* goes something like this. The search for causes is a fool's errand: it will go on forever, and can never be definitive. Instead of an endless, wandering search for causes, Howard thought, we should focus on the present. Everyone has a hierarchy of values. Racism may well be one of them but it is unlikely to be the thing that anyone cares about most. Change the external requirements of daily life so that whites must engage in equal status contact with blacks in order to achieve their highest priorities, and over time, attitudes will change in response. (6)

After his discharge by Spelman College, Howard moved to Boston and found an academic livelihood in the Political Science department at Boston University.

Living in the Boston area and making one's living at a university there may not, for most people, be a formula for solidarity with the poor and oppressed. Howard made it that. After he had been at Boston University about fifteen years, the faculty, the secretaries and staff, and the librarians, all organized unions and with various grievances, and at different times, went on strike. Howard was co-chair of the strike committee of the faculty union. Like the workers of the Gdansk shipyard in Poland, he and a few other teachers urged fellow faculty members to stay on strike until the university administration agreed to a contract not only with themselves, but also with university secretaries, although to do so might be viewed as violation of the new faculty contract banning "sympathy strikes." (7)

Ten years later, when Howard decided to "retire," at the suggestion of his wife Roz he ended his last class half an hour early and together with a hundred students joined a picket line of workers at the university School of Nursing who were protesting an administration decision to close the school because it was not making enough money. (8)

After Howard left the South, the two great themes of his later years were, on the one hand, *A People's History*, and on the other hand, his increasingly passionate and comprehensive opposition to United States imperialism and to war.

Howard did not invent the term "people's history." (9) Nor did he invent panoramic history of the United States drawn primarily from secondary sources. I can remember the excitement with which, as a high-school student, I read *The Rise of American Civilization* by Charles and Mary Beard. Academic historians are still catching up with their idea that the Civil War was a "second American Revolution."

A People's History is not mere popularization. In *A People's History* Howard presents a snapshot of labor history in the 1930s consistent with what he had written about the Ludlow strike. Far from celebrating the advent of the CIO in the manner of most labor historians, these pages offer a minority opinion parallel to that of Jeremy Brecher in his book *Strike!*, Marty Glaberman, Stan Weir, and myself. Thus Howard writes:

> [I]t was rank-and-file strikes and insurgencies that pushed the union leadership, AFL and CIO, into action . . . . It was to stabilize the system in the face of labor unrest that the Wagner Act of 1935, setting up the National Labor Relations Board, had been passed . . . . The NLRB would set limits in economic conflict as voting did in political conflict. And . . . the workers' organization itself, the union, even a militant and aggressive union like the CIO, would channel the workers' insurrectionary energy into contracts, negotiations, union meetings, and try to minimize strikes, in order to build large, influential, even respectable organizations.
>
> The history of those years seems to support the argument of Richard Cloward and Frances Piven, in their book *Poor People's Movements*, that labor won most during its spontaneous uprisings, before the unions were recognized or well organized . . . . (10)

Finally, Howard's concluding vision of a revolt of the guards is no doubt Utopian. But I have personally experienced a situation in which predominantly black guards in a private prison, whom I helped to organize a little independent union, began to make common cause with an almost exclusively black prison population in opposition to white administrators. It was pretty exciting. The Corrections Corporation of America, the largest operator of private prisons in the country, took us seriously. Within a week after the guards' union won a NLRB election, the company began to close the place.

I consider Howard's greatest achievement between the appearance of *The Politics of History* in 1970 and the death of my beloved friend and comrade forty years later to be his many-sided assault on what William Appleman Williams called "empire as a way of life."

The young Howard Zinn emerged from the anti-Fascist politics of the Popular Front in the late 1930s to become a bombardier in World War II. He tells us in his autobiography how and why his outlook changed. (11) The bombing plane that drops its payload on human beings (most of them civilians and many of them children) whose suffering the plane crew never sees, or hears, or smells, came to represent for Howard the inevitable horror of all modern warfare. After Hiroshima, Howard came to repudiate "that bombing and all the others."(12)

His opening challenge to United States aggression was *Vietnam: The Logic of Withdrawal*, which appeared in 1967. Notice two things.

First, as with racial segregation, there is next to no attention to the cause of the Vietnam conflict. The rest of us were looking for offshore oil reserves, or tungsten deposits, to explain the disproportionate interest of the American ruling class in this small, impoverished country. Later, after the publication of the Pentagon Papers, as an expert witness Howard told juries that United States policy was shown to have been motivated by "tin, rubber, [and] oil."(13) In *Vietnam: The Logic of Withdrawal*, however, Howard was single-minded in trying to end the war, not explain it.

Second, as with racial segregation, there is a lingering hope, perhaps based on President Truman's desegregation order, that the federal government can be induced to change its mind. This took the form of an imaginary speech by President Johnson ending United States intervention.

At journey's end Howard Zinn had become convinced that only direct action from below, by American soldiers who refuse to fight, can end United States imperialism. By the time of his death Howard was passionately urging that the civil disobedience he had first defended in the context of racial segregation should be practiced by members of the United States military.

Howard was never comfortable with joining organizations or with labels for his forthright affirmations. As an alternative to mass killing, he proposed action that is "focused, controlled, intervening between victims and the evil they face without creating more victims," and viewed finding such a substitute for war as "the central issue of our time." Another formulation advocated nonviolence in the form of "underground movements, strikes, general strikes, noncompliance." (14)

But Howard was not a pacifist. He rejected war under any conceivable set of modern circumstances, because of what he considered its inevitable impact on innocent civilians, especially children. No such war could be just.

Similarly, he was not an anarchist. But it would be hard to find anyone, anywhere, who more passionately advocated disbelief in the official pronouncements of all governments. One recent statement was this from 2005:

> . . . [W]e cannot depend on the governments of the world to abolish war because they and the economic interests they represent benefit from war. Therefore, we, the people of the world, must take up the challenge. And although we do not command armies, we do not have great treasuries of wealth, there is one crucial fact that gives us enormous power: the governments of the world cannot wage war without the participation of the people. Albert Einstein understood this simple fact. Horrified by the carnage of World War I in which ten million people died in the battle fields of Europe, Einstein said: "Wars will stop when men refuse to fight."

This is our challenge, to bring the world to the point where men will refuse to fight, and governments will be helpless to wage war. (15)

After Howard's death, "Courage to Resist," a network of persons in the military who refuse further service, circulated a flier with the following quotation from him: "As a veteran myself I know how difficult it is to break out of the stranglehold the military has on one's mind, and how much courage that takes." (16)

To conclude: When a soldier falls in battle, we pick up his gun. When a comrade dies in the struggle for nonviolent revolution, we try to pick up his dreams.

There is a scene in Howard's SNCC book about the release of a battered civil rights worker from jail in Hattiesburg, Mississippi. Present were two lawyers, dressed impeccably; Howard Zinn, moderately presentable; and Oscar Chase, "his face swollen, his clothes bloody." The FBI agent came out of his office and surveyed the four. Then he asked, "Who was it got the beating?" (17)

Is this a description of academic history? Surely we too need to be more precise and explicit in distinguishing victims from executioners. And then, remembering Howard, we need to do something about it.

Howard Zinn, *presente*.

NOTES

(1) I base my description on "The Ludlow Massacre," appearing in Howard Zinn, *The Politics of History*, 1990 edition (Urbana and Chicago: University of Illinois Press, 1970, 1990), pp. 79-101. Howard's biographer says that the essay sets forth "the essence" of the M.A. thesis. Davis D. Joyce, *Howard Zinn: A Radical American Vision* (Amherst, N.Y.: Prometheus Books, 2003), p. 39. Introducing a reprinting of his Ludlow essay as it appeared in *The Politics of History*, Howard says that the Ludlow massacre came to his attention in two ways, "first in a song by Woodie Guthrie called 'The Ludlow Massacre,' then in a chapter of the book by Samuel Yellen, *American Labor Struggles*, written in 1936." Howard Zinn, *The Zinn Reader: Writings on Disobedience and Democracy* (New York: Seven Stories Press, 1997), p. 183.

(2) Howard Zinn, *You Can't Be Neutral on a Moving Train: A Personal History of Our Times* (Boston: Beacon Press, 1994), pp. 170-171, 175-177.

(3) *The Politics of History*, p. 79. In a column for The *Progressive* magazine, written near the end of his life, Howard reiterated that the Ludlow massacre was "still absent from mainstream history books." Howard Zinn, *A Power Governments Cannot Suppress* (San Francisco: City Lights Books, 2007), p. 101.

(4) *The Politics of History*, p. 100.

(5) *Ibid.*, p. 49.

(6) Howard Zinn, *The Southern Mystique* (New York: Alfred A. Knopf, 1964), pp. 7 (cause "not only baffles people, but, worse, immobilizes them"), 9 (except as an academic exercise, there is no need "to probe the fog that inescapably shrouds the philosophical question of causation"), 11 ("there is a magical and omnipotent dispeller of the mystery; it is contact"), 18 ("you first change the way people behave . . . in order to transform the environment which is the ultimate determinant of the way they think"), 93 ("the universal detergent for race prejudice is contact—massive, prolonged, equal, and intimate contact").

(7) *You Can't Be Neutral*, pp. 190-191.

(8) *Ibid.*, pp. 202-203.

(9) A young man named Harvey Wasserman had previously sent Howard Zinn a manuscript entitled a "People's History" of the period between 1860 and 1920. Harvey Wasserman, "How the great Howard Zinn made all our lives better," e-mail, Jan. 28, 2010.

(10) Howard Zinn, *A People's History of the United States, 1492-Present, Twentieth Anniversary Edition* (New York: HarperCollins, 1999), pp. 399-402. In Howard Zinn and Anthony Arnove, *Voices of a People's History of the United States* (New York: Seven Stories Press, 2004), pp. 332-340, 345-349, three "voices" from the organization of the CIO are presented. All are rank-and-file workers. All are women. They are Genora Dollinger, who organized the Women's Emergency Brigade in Flint, and two of the three "union maids" (Vicky Starr [Stella Nowicki] and Sylvia Woods) whose memories are reported in *Rank and File: Personal Histories by Working-Class Organizers*, ed. Alice and Staughton Lynd, third edition (New York: Monthly Review Press, 1988). Note, too, that Howard's own experience as a rank-and-file union member, first as a warehouse worker while he was at graduate school, later as a professor seeking to act in solidarity with non-academic staff at Boston University, was to be "more left than the union." *You Can't Be Neutral*, pp. 180, 101. (16) Howard Zinn, *You Can't Be Neutral*, p. 11.

(11) See especially You Can't Be Neutral, pp. 94-95 (fellow airman who told Howard that World War II was an "imperialist" war), 92-94 and 97 (experience in bombing the French town of Royan with napalm when the German soldiers there were waiting to surrender).

(12) *Ibid.*, p. 11.

(13) *Ibid.*, pp. 155, 161.

(14) *Ibid.*, pp. 100-101; Howard Zinn, *Terrorism and War* (New York: Seven Stories Press, 2002), p. 23.

(15) Howard Zinn, *Just War* (San Giovanni, Italy: Edizioni Charta, 2005), p. 14.

(16) E-mail from Courage to Resist, Feb. 3, 2010. To the same effect, Howard Zinn, Introduction to David Cortright, *Soldiers in Revolt: GI Resistance During the Vietnam War*, updated edition (Chicago: Haymarket Books, 2005), reprinted in Howard Zinn, *A Power Governments Cannot Suppress* (San Francisco: City Lights Books, 2007), pp. 173-177. Other relevant essays in this book, which reprints columns Howard wrote for *The Progressive* magazine, are: "World War II: The Good War," pp. 43-47; "Learning from Hiroshima," pp. 49-55; "Afghanistan," pp. 77-90; on refusal to fight in Vietnam, "Henry David Thoreau," p. 137; "The Enemy is War," pp. 189-197.

(17) Howard Zinn, *SNCC: The New Abolitionists*, second edition (Boston: Beacon Press, 1965), p. 117.

Howard Zinn, Presente*

by Staughton Lynd

*Presented at a 2013 conference of Historians Against the War in Towson, Maryland and at the 2013 OAH Convention in San Francisco

In order to be a conscientious objector in the United States one must declare an objection to all wars, and make that objection on the basis of religious training and belief. The government's position is that the only conscientious objection recognized by law is pacifism. But at the end of World War II, the victorious Allies sentenced defeated opponents to death for "war crimes," "crimes against humanity," and "crimes against peace" in a particular war.

Representatives of the United States at Nuremburg such as Robert Jackson, a justice of the United States Supreme Court, and prosecutor Telford Taylor, declared that henceforth the conduct of United States military personnel would also be evaluated on the basis of the Nuremburg principles. But when Dr. Howard Levy during the Vietnam War, or Camillo Mejia and Kevin Benderman in the wars against Iraq, sought to refuse further military service on the basis of the Nuremburg principles, Dr. Levy's claim was rejected by the United States Supreme Court, and Mejia and Benderman were court martialed and imprisoned.

The law of conscientious objection in the United States is intended to accommodate members of certain small Protestant sects, such as the Amish, Hutterites, and Quakers. Moreover, would-be conscientious objectors are unlikely to have their applications approved unless they have registered objection before entering the military and thus before actually experiencing the horrors of war. These arrangements ensure that, in a volunteer army, there will never be more than a handful of conscientious objectors. The process is an example of what Herbert Marcuse called "repressive tolerance."

Howard Zinn is the paradigmatic conscientious objector to war on the basis, not of pacifism, but of his experience as a soldier. Although this has sometimes been described as the outlook of "particular war objection," Howard came to feel that no conceivable modern war could be just because the technology with which any modern war would be fought made inevitable the systematic commission of war crimes. The former bombardier concluded that warfare as it is presently practiced requires one human being to cause bombs to be dropped on other human beings, always including civilians and, especially, children, from a height or distance such that the bombardier cannot see, or hear, or smell, the consequences of these actions.

This was a position that Howard came to gradually. He grew up in Brooklyn at a time when many Communist Party members and sympathizers lived in that part of New York City. Howard's teen-age convictions must be understood in that context. In 1935 the worldwide Communist movement embraced a strategy that characterized fascism as the main danger to humankind. Howard and his biographer Martin Duberman tell us that as he learned about fascism Howard came to detest it.

But from 1939 (when Howard was seventeen) to 1941 the Communist movement also put forward the view that the war declared by Great Britain and France against Germany in September 1939 was a "phony war." Antiwar advocacy was widespread. A book that greatly influenced Howard was *Johnny Get Your Gun* by Dalton Trumbo, in which a young man goes to war and becomes a quadriplegic. After the German invasion of the Soviet Union, the Communist Party once more single-mindedly supported military resistance to fascism. In one of my last conversations with Howard he remarked bitterly that during World War II the Party in the United States prevented the re-issuance of Trumbo's novel.

At the time, though, Howard himself initially became a fervent supporter of the Allied war effort. He had gone to work in a shipyard making vessels for the Navy. In 1943 he gave up that job and volunteered for the Air Force. So determined was he to get into combat that, he writes, "twice . . . I traded places with other bombardiers to get on the short list for overseas." (*You Can't Be Neutral*, p. 90.)

There are many clues to what led the young bombardier to begin to become a leading opponent of United States wars.

The Socialist Workers Party had a policy of sending its members into the armed forces to "win over" other soldiers. Howard became friends with a gunner on another bomber crew. One day his friend said, "You know, this is not a war against fascism . . . . It's an imperialist war." Startled, Howard asked him, "Then why are you here?" The other replied, "To talk to guys like you." Two weeks after that conversation Howard's friend was shot down and killed. (*Neutral*, pp. 94-95.)

A second critical experience was Howard's participation in bombing a French town named Royan. A few thousand German soldiers had gathered there, waiting to surrender when the war ended. The ostensible reason for the bombing mission was to "take them out." But the weapon chosen was thirty one-hundred-pound canisters of jellied gasoline, or as Howard later learned to call it, napalm. Many French civilians were also killed in this unnecessary bombing run. Its real purpose, Howard thought for the rest of his life, was to try out a new weapon. (*Neutral*, pp. 92-93.)

Finally, just at the end of World War II, Howard learned that his two closest friends in the Air Force, with whom he had lived through basic training and various phases of flight school, had been killed. Howard writes that he dreamed about them. He felt that he had been given the undeserved gift of fifty years of life denied to Joe and Ed. He owed them something. (*Neutral*, pp. 11-12.)

And so, when Howard left military service, he collected "some photos, old navigation logs, and some other momentos, my Air Medal and ribbons with two battle stars, put them into a folder and without thinking wrote on the folder, 'Never again.'" (*Neutral*, p. 95.)

I knew Howard intimately a little more than fifteen years later. He was excited about Joseph Heller's novel, *Catch-22*. Its hero, Yossarian, says that in the military the "enemy" is whoever wants to do you serious harm, and that many of these enemies are a soldier's superior officers.

Consider the years from 1965, when President Johnson reneged on his campaign pledges and escalated war in Vietnam, to 2010 when

Howard died. Among my impressions of Howard during these years are the following:

1. He wasn't particular interested in the causes of war, in Vietnam or anywhere else. As he explained in *The Politics of History*, it seemed to Howard that the search for causes is inconclusive and therefore unending.
2. He placed less and less faith in national governments. Perhaps impressed with President Truman's action of ending racial segregation in the military by executive order, in 1964 Howard labored mightily to induce President Johnson to appoint special marshals to protect civil rights workers in the South. In later years Howard would say, simply, never trust a national government to tell the truth or to act appropriately.
3. Howard's last public address was delivered on November 11, the date that when Howard and I were young was called "Armistice Day."

The text of this speech is now available in a collection entitled *Howard Zinn Speaks*, edited by Anthony Arnove. It is entitled "Three Holy Wars." Of course Howard meant, unholy wars. The three unholy wars are the American Revolution, the Civil War, and World War II.

In this address Howard criticized what are generally viewed—by historians, by the Left, and by the general public—as the three great people's triumphs of our national history. How, Howard asked, can one criticize events that brought about independence, an end to slavery, and the defeat of fascism? He proceeded to do so.

First, the Revolution. The 25,000 persons who died would be equivalent to two and a half million today. "[W]e just assume that everybody benefited from independence," Howard went on. But they didn't. It wasn't easy to recruit an army. "People don't naturally rush to war. You have to seduce them, you have to bribe them or coerce them. Some people think it's natural for people to go to war. Not at all." Many Americans opposed the war for independence, especially when they found out that the rich could escape conscription by paying a sum of money. Those who went into the army were often, as we would say today, "stop lossed": in Howard's words, "when their time was up they were told, no, they had to stay."

Slaves didn't benefit from the Revolution. Native Americans lost ground—literally as well as figuratively—because there was no longer a British proclamation attempting to halt westward expansion at the crest of the Appalachians.

And Howard asks, was there a way to become independent without a war? Canada did it. It took Canada longer than the United States to become independent, but. "[s]ometimes it takes longer if you don't want to kill." And sometimes you end up with something better, like Canada's universal health insurance.

Howard understood the number of Civil War deaths to be 600,000, although recent analysis of census reports suggests that the figure may have been 750,000. He pointed to the ambiguous result for the slaves: they were free, but they did not receive the forty acres and a mule that would have given that freedom a foundation. (Where they were given land, on the Sea Islands off the South Carolina coast, they had to give it back.).

And again Howard asks, Might the same result have been achieved without a war? There is no way to be sure, he concedes. But, he remarks, as he did about Canada's path to independence from Great Britain, "Slavery was ended [everywhere else] in the Western Hemisphere without a bloody civil war."

Then, of course, we come to World War II, Howard's war, the "good war." Howard states that, beside the horrors of Hiroshima and Nagasaki, 600,000 German civilians were killed by bombing raids and a total of 50 million people died in that war.

Howard ends with what became his characteristic theme at the end of his life, as it is of mine: "When soldiers refuse to fight . . . wars can't go on."

4. Finally, I believe Howard Zinn recognized and resurrected the main theme of American radicalism between the Revolution and World War I. In his autobiography, he wrote that he interpreted the Declaration of Independence "to include men, women, and children all over the world, who have a right to life not to be taken away by their own government or by ours." (*Neutral*, p. 3.) And Howard ended a speech entitled "The Myth of American Exceptionalism," by quoting the masthead of William Lloyd Garrison's antislavery newspaper, *The Liberator*: "My country is the world. My countrymen are mankind." (*Howard Zinn Speaks*, p. 184.)

Lucasville Prison Uprising

by Staughton Lynd
Presented at a conference on Re-Examining Lucasville,
April 19-21, 2013, Columbus Ohio

Our focus this morning has been a detailed discussion of what happened before and during the eleven days and in the trials that followed. My comments are intended to build a bridge between that analysis and the broader perspectives that will be offered this afternoon. I will divide my remarks in four parts.

First, I shall recall the three biggest prison rebellions in recent United States history. I will suggest that while we are just beginning to build a movement outside the walls of both prisons and courtrooms, there are particular aspects of the Lucasville events that help to explain why that has been so hard.

Second, I will make the case that, despite appearances, Ohio's prison administration was at least as responsible as were the prisoners for the ten deaths during the occupation of L block.

Third, I shall describe the manipulation by means of which the State of Ohio induced a leader of the uprising to become an informer and to attribute responsibility for the murder of hostage Officer Robert Vallandingham to others. I shall add that to this day the State says it does not know who the hands-on killers were.

Finally, and very briefly, because I recognize this will be the agenda for tomorrow morning, I will ask: What is to be done?

Three Prison Uprisings

There have been three major prison uprisings in the United States during the past half century.

The first and best-known rebellion was at Attica in western New York State in September 1971. Prisoners occupied a recreation yard. After three days, agents of the state assaulted the area, guns blazing. The prisoners had killed three prisoners and a guard. The state's assault resulted in the deaths of 29 more prisoners and an additional 10 guards whom the prisoners were holding as hostages.

Initially the State of New York, including Governor Nelson Rockefeller, claimed that the hostage officers who died in the yard had their throats cut by the prisoners in rebellion. A courageous medical examiner said, No, the officers all died of bullet wounds. And only one side in the conflict, or massacre, had guns.

Because the brazen cover story of the authorities was so soon and so dramatically refuted, the prosecution of prisoners at Attica never got far off the ground. On December 31, 1976, a little more than five years after the events at the prison, New York governor Carey declared by executive order an amnesty for all participants in the insurrection. He stated in part:

Attica has been a tragedy of immeasurable proportions, unalterably affecting countless lives. Too many families have grieved, too many have suffered deprivations, too many have lived their lives in uncertainty waiting for the long nightmare to end. For over five years and with hundreds of thousands of dollars and countless man-hours we have followed the path of investigation and accusation . . . . To continue in this course, I believe, would merely prolong the agony with no better hope of a just and abiding conclusion.

The governor concluded by saying that his actions should not be understood to imply "a lack of culpability for the conduct at issue." Rather, Governor Carey stated, "these actions are in recognition that there does exist a larger wrong which transcends the wrongful acts of individuals."

In 1980 a second major uprising occurred at the state prison in Santa Fe, New Mexico. Again there were numerous deaths, but all 33 homicides resulted from prisoners killing other prisoners. No officers were murdered. No prisoner was sentenced to death.

Finally we come to the Southern Ohio Correctional Facility in Lucasville in 1993. In trying to understand the tangle of events we call "Lucasville" one confronts: a prisoner body of more than 1800, a majority of them black men from Ohio's inner cities, guarded by correctional officers largely recruited from the entirely, or almost entirely, white community in Scioto County; a prison administration determined to suppress dissent after the murder of an educator in 1990; an eleven-day occupation by more than four hundred men of a major part of the Lucasville prison; ten homicides, all committed by prisoners, including the murder of hostage officer Robert Vallandingham; dialogue between the parties ending in a peaceful surrender; and about fifty prosecutions, resulting in five capital convictions and numerous other sentences, some of them likely to last for the remainder of a prisoner's life.

The task for defense lawyers, and for a community campaign demanding reconsideration, is more difficult than at Attica or Santa Fe. At Attica, 10 of the 11 officers who died were killed by agents of the State. At Santa Fe, only prisoners were killed. Lucasville presents a distinct challenge: the killing of a single hostage correctional officer murdered by prisoners in rebellion.

Who Is To Blame?

In a summary booklet Alice and I have produced, entitled *Layers of Injustice*, we argue that the Lucasville prisoners in L block, considered collectively, and the State of Ohio share responsibility for the tragedy of April 1993. Both sides contributed to what happened. Events spun out of control. Neither side intended what occurred.

The collective responsibility of prisoners in L-block seems self-evident. Ten men were killed. The victims were unarmed and helpless. In contrast to what happened at Attica, all ten victims were killed by prisoners.

However, Muslim prisoner Reginald Williams, a witness for the State in the Lucasville trials, testified that the hope of the group that planned the 1993 occupation was to carry out a brief, essentially peaceful, attention-getting action "to get someone from the central office to come down and address our concerns" (*State v. Were I* at 1645), "to barricade ourselves in L-6 until we can get someone from Columbus to discuss" alternative means of doing the TB tests (*State v. Sanders* at 2129.) Siddique Abdullah Hasan, supposed by the State to have planned and led the action, said the same thing to the Associated Press within the past two weeks.

Since the prisoners, whatever their initial intentions, nonetheless carried out the homicides, the responsibility of the State is less obvious. Here are some of the main reasons I believe that the State of Ohio shares responsibility for what happened at Lucasville in 1993

1. In 1989, Warden Terry Morris asked the legislative oversight committee of the Ohio General Assembly to prepare a survey of conditions at the Southern Ohio Correctional Facility in Lucasville. The Correctional Institution Inspection Committee received letters from 427 prisoners and interviewed more than 100. Such was the state of disarray in 1989 that, four years before the 1993 uprising, the CIIC reported that prisoners "relayed fears and predictions of a major disturbance unlike any ever seen in Ohio prison history."
2. After the murder of educator Beverly Jo Taylor in 1990, a new warden was appointed. Warden Arthur Tate instituted what he called "Operation Shakedown." A striking example of the pervasive repression reported by prisoners is that telephone communication between prisoners and the outside world was limited to one, five minute, outgoing telephone call per year.
3. The single feature of life at Lucasville that the CIIC found most troublesome was the prison administration's use of prisoner informants, or "snitches." Warden Tate, "King Arthur" as the prisoners called him, expanded the use of snitches. In 1991 the warden addressed a letter to all prisoners and visitors in which he provided a special mailing address to which alleged violations of "laws and rules of this institution" could be reported. Six alleged snitches, a majority of the persons murdered during the rebellion, were killed in the first hours of the disturbance.
4. The immediate cause or trigger of the rebellion was Warden Tate's insistence on testing for TB by injecting a substance containing phenol, which a substantial number of Muslim prisoners believed to be prohibited by their religion. Alternative means of testing for TB by use of X rays or a sputum test were available and had been used at Mansfield Correctional Institution. In its post-surrender report, the correctional officers' labor union stated that Warden Tate was "unnecessarily confrontational" in his response to the Muslim prisoners' concern about TB testing using phenol.

5. Before Warden Tate departed for the Easter weekend on Good Friday, three of his administrators advised against his plan to lock the prison down and forcibly inject prisoners who refused TB shots. The warden did not adequately alert the reduced staff who would be on duty as to the volatile state of affairs. Slow response to the initial occupation of L block let pass an early opportunity to end the rebellion without loss of life. It was two hours after the insurgency began before Warden Tate was notified. The safewells at the end of each pod in L block, to which correctional officers retreated as they had been instructed, turned out to have been constructed without the prescribed steel stanchions and were easily penetrated.

6. Sergeant Howard Hudson, who was in the administration control booth during the eleven days and was offered by prosecutors as a so-called "summary witness," conceded in his trial testimony that the State of Ohio deliberately stalled when prisoners tried to end the standoff by negotiation. Hudson testified in Hasan's case: "The basic principle in these situations . . . is to buy time . . . . [T]he more time that goes on the greater the chances for a peaceful resolution to the situation." This assumption proved—to use an unfortunate phrase—to be dead wrong.

7. By cutting off water and electricity to the occupied cell block on April 12, the State created a new cause of grievance. The prisoners' concern to get back what they had at the outset of the disturbance became the sticking point in unsuccessful negotiations to end the standoff before Officer Vallandingham was murdered.

8. On the morning of April14, spokeswoman Tessa Unwin made a statement to the press on behalf of the authorities. Ms. Unwin was asked to comment on a message written on a sheet that was hung out of an L block window threatening to kill a hostage officer. Rather than responding "No comment," she stated: "It's a standard threat. It's nothing new . . . They've been threatening things like this from the beginning." According to several prisoners in L block and to hostage officer Larry Dotson, this statement inflamed sentiment among the prisoners who were listening on battery-powered radios. In the judgment of the officers' union, in their report on the disturbance:

As anyone familiar with the process and language of negotiations would know, this kind of public discounting of the inmate threats practically guaranteed a hostage death.

When an official DR&C spokesperson publicly discounted the inmate threats as bluffing, the inmates were almost forced to kill or maim a hostage to maintain or regain their perceived bargaining strength.

9. In 2010, documentary filmmaker Derrick Jones interviewed Daniel Hogan, who prosecuted Robb and Skatzes and is now a state court judge. Hogan told Jones on tape: "I don't know that we will ever know who hands-on killed the corrections officer, Vallandingham." Later Mr. Jones asked former prosecutor Hogan: "When it comes to Officer Vallandingham, who killed him?" Judge Hogan replied: "I don't know. And I don't think we'll ever know." Nonetheless, four spokespersons and supposed leaders of the uprising have been found guilty of the officer's aggravated murder, and sentenced to death.

Who Did Kill Officer Vallandingham?

With the help of Attorney Niki Schwartz, three prisoner representatives accepted a 21 point agreement and a peaceful surrender followed. The agreement stated in point 6, "Administrative discipline and criminal proceedings will be fairly and impartially administered without bias against individuals or groups." Point 14 added, "There will be no retaliatory actions taken toward any inmate or groups of inmates."

The raw intent of the State to violate these understandings was made clear during and immediately after the surrender. Inmate Emanuel Newell, who had almost been killed by the rebelling prisoners, was carried out of L block on a stretcher. A trooper asked him, "What did you see Skatzes do? Newell and John Fryman, who had been assaulted by the insurgents and left for dead, were put in the Lucasville infirmary. Both were approached by representatives of the State. Fryman remembered:

They made it clear they wanted the leaders. They wanted to prosecute Hasan, George Skatzes, Lavelle, Jason Robb, and another Muslim. They had not yet begun their investigation but they knew they wanted those leaders. I joked with them and said, "You basically don't care what I say as long as it's against these guys." They said, "Yeah, that's it."

Newell named the men who had interrogated him: Lieutenant Root, Sergeant Hudson, and Troopers McGough and Sayers. According to Newell:

> These officers said, "We want Skatzes. We want Lavelle. We want Hasan." They also said, "We know they were leaders . . . . We want to burn their ass. We want to put them in the electric chair for murdering Officer Vallandingham."

With the same motivation, the prosecutors pursued a more sophisticated strategy. ODRC Director Reginald Wilkinson put it this way in an article that he co-authored with his associate Thomas Stickrath for the *Corrections Management Quarterly*:

According to Special Prosecutor Mark Piepmeier, his staff targeted a few gang leaders . . . . Thirteen months into the investigation, a primary riot provocateur agreed to talk about Officer Vallandingham's death . . . . His testimony led to death sentences for riot leaders Carlos Sanders, Jason Robb, James Were, and George Skatzes.

The so-called primary riot provocateur was prisoner Anthony Lavelle, leader of the Black Gangster Disciples, who, along with Hasan and Robb, had negotiated the surrender agreement.

How did the State induce Lavelle not only to talk, but to say what the prosecution desired?

During the winter of 1993-1994, Hasan, Lavelle, and Skatzes were housed in adjacent cells at the Chillicothe Correctional Institution. On April 6, 1994, Skatzes was taken to a room where he found Sergeant Hudson, Trooper McGough of the Highway Patrol, and two prosecutors. This was the third such occasion and, as twice before, Skatzes said that he did not wish to continue the interview, and turned to go back to his cell in the North Hole.

What happened next, according to Skatzes, was that Warden Ralph Coyle entered the room and said that Central Office did not want Skatzes to go back to the North Hole. Skatzes protested vehemently that this would make him look like a snitch. Coyle was adamant and Skatzes was led away to a new location.

Back in the North Hole, Lavelle reacted exactly as Skatzes feared. Lavelle wrote a letter to Jason Robb that became an exhibit in Robb's trial: "Jason: I am forced to write you and relate a few things that happen down here lately. With much sadness I will give you the raw deal, your brother George has done a vanishing act on us . . . . On Wednesday, April 6, 1994 G. said about 8:00 a.m. that he had a lawyer visit . . . . Now to be short and simple, he failed to return that day. Today they came and packed up his property which leads me to one conclusion that he has chose to be a cop."

Later, Lavelle himself testified that he turned State's evidence because he thought he would go to Death Row if he did not. This was an accurate assessment. Prosecutor Hogan told a trial court judge at sidebar that his colleague Prosecutor Stead had told Lavelle, Either you are going to be my witness or I'm going to try to kill you. According to the testimony under oath of prisoner Anthony Odom, who celled across from Lavelle at the time Lavelle entered into his plea agreement, Lavelle "said he was gonna cop out [be]cause the prosecutor was sweating him, trying to hit him with a murder charge . . . . He said he was going to tell them what they wanted to hear."

Lavelle was understandably concerned that the prosecutor might hit him with a murder charge because it is overwhelmingly likely thatit was, in fact, he who coordinated Officer Vallandingham's murder. I have laid out the evidence in my book and in an article in the *Capital University Law Review*. Briefly,

Three members of the Black Gangster Disciples stated under oath that Lavelle tried to recruit them for a death squad after Ms. Unwin's statement on April 14;

> Sean Davis, who slept in L-1 as Lavelle did, testified that when he awoke on the morning of April 15, he heard Lavelle telling Stacey Gordon that he was going to kill a guard to which Gordon replied that he would clean up afterward;
>
> The late James Bell a.k.a. Nuruddin executed an affidavit before his death to the effect that Lavelle had left the morning meeting on April 15 furious that the Muslims and Aryans were unwilling to kill a hostage officer;

Three prisoners saw Lavelle and two other Disciples come down the L—block corridor from L-1 and go into L-6, leaving a few minutes later;

James Were, on guard duty in L-6 and thereby an eye witness to the murder, went to L-1 when he learned that the action had not been approved by other riot leaders and knocked Lavelle to the ground. Willie Johnson and Eddie Moss heard were explicitly blame Lavelle for the killing;

Two older and, in my opinion, reliable convicts, Leroy Elmore and the late Roy Donald, say that on April 15 Lavelle told each of them in so many words that he had had the guard killed.

Unlike prisoners who testified for the State, the twelve men whose evidence I have summarized received no benefits for coming forward and, in fact, risked retaliation from other inmates by doing so. No jury has ever heard their collective narrative.

What is to be Done?

So, what can we do?

The first task is to make it possible for the men condemned to death and life in prison to tell their stories, on camera, in face-to-face interviews with representatives of the media.

For twenty years the State of Ohio, through both its Columbus office of communications and individual wardens, has denied requests for media access to all prisoners convicted of illegal acts during the 11-day occupation. Indeed, in the 11-day occupation itself, one of the prisoners' persistent demands was for the opportunity to tell their story to the world. In telephone calls to the authorities during the first night of the occupation, prisoner representatives proposed a telephone interview with one media representative, or a live interview with a designated TV channel, in exchange for the release of one hostage correctional officer. At 7:00 a.m. on Monday, April 12 the prisoners in rebellion broke off telephone negotiations, demanding local and national news coverage before any hostage release.

In the late morning of April 12, George Skatzes volunteered to go out on the yard, accompanied by Cecil Allen, carrying an enormous white flag of truce. The men asked for access to the media already camped outside the prison walls.

When on April 15 and 16 the prisoners released hostage officers Darrold Clark and Anthony Demons, what did they ask for and get in return? The opportunity for one spokesperson, Skatzes, to make a radio address and for another, Muslim Stanley Cummings, to speak on TV the next morning.

Now the Lucasville prisoners are again knocking on the door of the State, hunger striking, crying out against their isolation from the dialogue of civic society. They ask, Why are we being kept incommunicado? What is the State afraid of?

I urge all present not to be distracted by official talk about alternative means of communication. The state tells us that the men condemned to death can write letters and make telephone calls. But the media access that these prisoners seek is the kind of exchange that can occur in courtroom cross-examination. The condemned are saying to us, Before you kill me, give me a chance to join with you in trying to figure out what actually occurred.

These are not homicides like that of which Mumia Abu Jamal is accused or that for which Troy Davis was executed: homicides with one decedent, one alleged perpetrator, and half a dozen witnesses. This is an immense tangle of events. There is no objective evidence except for the testimony of the medical examiners, which repeatedly contradicted the claims of the prosecution. Very few physical objects remain in existence. The medical examiner testified that David Sommers was killed by a single massive blow with an object like a bat. A bloody baseball bat was found near the body of David Sommers. Special Prosecutor Mark Piepmeier ordered the bat to be destroyed.

We need media access to the Lucasville Five and their companions not just to perceive them as human beings, but to determine the truth. George Skatzes and Aaron Jefferson were tried in separate trials and each was convicted of striking the single massive blow that killed Mr. Sommers. Eric Girdy has confessed to being one of the three killers of Earl Elder, using a shank made of glass from the mirror in the officers' restroom, and slivers of glass were found in one of the lethal wounds and on the nearby floor. Girdy has insisted under oath that Skatzes had nothing to do with the murder; yet the State, while accepting Girdy's confession, has not vacated the judgment against Skatzes. Hasan and Namir were found Not Guilty of killing Bruce Harris yet Stacey Gordon, who admitted to being one of the killers, is on the street. The trial court judge in Keith LaMar's trial refused to direct the prosecution to turn over to counsel for the defense the transcripts of all interviews conducted by the Highway Patrol with potential witnesses of the homicides for which LaMar was convicted, and LaMar is now closest to death of the Five. Jason Robb did nothing to cause the death of Officer Vallandingham except to attend an inconclusive meeting also attended by Anthony Lavelle, but only Robb was sentenced to death.

These things are not right, not just, not fair. The men facing death and life imprisonment for their alleged actions in April 1993 need to be full participants in the truth-seeking process. That is why, to repeat, I believe that our first task following this gathering is to make it possible for these men to tell their stories, on camera, in face-to-face interviews with representatives of the media. Journalists, for example from campus newspapers, who wish precise information as to how to request interviews should contact me.

A Letter to Other Occupiers

February 28, 2012
by Staughton Lynd

Greetings. I write from Niles, Ohio, near Youngstown. I take part in Occupy Youngstown (OY). I was asked to make some "keynote" remarks on the occasion of OY's first public meeting on October 15, 2011. I am a member of the legal team that filed suit after our tent and burn barrel were confiscated on November 10-11. I am helping to create the OY Free University where working groups explore a variety of future projects.

I do not write to comment on recent events in Oakland. Our younger daughter lived for a few years in a co-operative house situated on the border between Berkeley and Oakland. For part of that time Martha worked at a public school in Oakland where most of the children were Hispanic. A can company wanted to take the school's recreation yard. In protest, parents courageously kept their children out of school, causing the school's public funding to drop precipitously. As I understand it, in the end the parents prevailed and got a new rec yard.

That was many years ago. It sticks in my mind as an example of the sort of activity, reaching out to the communities in which we live, that I hope Occupiers are undertaking all over the country.

I

Every local Occupy movement of which I am aware has begun to explore the terrain beyond the downtown public square, asking, what is to be done next?

This is as it should be and we need to be gentle with ourselves and one another, recognizing the special difficulties of this task. The European middle class, before taking state power from feudal governments, built a network of new institutions within the shell of the old society: free cities, guilds, Protestant congregations, banks and corporations, and finally, parliaments. It appears to be much more difficult to construct such prefigurative enclaves within capitalism, a more tightly-knit social fabric.

I sense that, because of this difficulty in building long-term institutions, in much of the Occupy universe there is now an emphasis on protests, marches, "days" for this or that, symbolic but temporary occupations, and other tactics of the moment, rather than on a strategy of building ongoing new institutions and dual power.

I have a particular concern about the impending confrontation in Chicago in May between the forces of Occupy and capitalist globalization. My fears are rooted in a history that may seem to many of you irrelevant. If so, stroke my fevered brow and assure me that you have no intention of letting Occupy crash and burn in the way that both the Student Nonviolent Coordinating Committee (SNCC) and Students for a Democratic Society (SDS) did at the end of the Sixties.

II

Here, in brief, is the history that I pray we will not repeat.

In August 1964, rank-and-file African Americans in the Mississippi Freedom Democratic Party (MFDP), staff of SNCC, and many summer volunteers, traveled to the convention of the national Democratic Party in Atlantic City to demand that the inter-racial delegates of the MFDP should be seated in place of the all-white delegates from the "regular," segregationist Mississippi Democrats. It was an apocalyptic moment, made especially riveting by the televised testimony of Fannie Lou Hamer.

But politically speaking, many who made the trip from the Deep South never found their way back there. A variety of causes were at work but one was that it seemed tedious to return from the mountaintop experience up North to the apparently more humdrum day-to-day movement work in Mississippi. The so-called Congressional Challenge that followed the traumatic events in Atlantic

City caused many activists to continue to spend time away from local communities in which they had been living and working.

Bear with me if I continue this ancient Movement history.

In November 1965, there was a gathering in Washington DC of representatives from a myriad of ad hoc student groups formed to oppose the Vietnam war. During the weeks before this occasion several friends warned me that different Left groups were preparing to do battle for control of the new antiwar movement. I assured them that their fears were needless: that kind of thing might have happened in the 1930s, but we were a **new** Left, committed to listening to one another and to learning from our collective experience.

I was wrong. From the opening gavel, both Communists and Trotskyists sought to take control of the new activist network. In the process they seriously disillusioned many young persons who, perhaps involved in their first political protest, had come long distances in the hope of creating a common front against the war.

Paul Booth of SDS called this meeting "the crazy convention." I remember sleeping on the floor of somebody's apartment next to Dave Dellinger as the two of us sought to refocus attention on what was happening in Vietnam. I recall pleading near the end of the occasion with members of the Young Socialist Alliance (YSA) to be allowed into a locked hotel room where, apparently having lost on the convention floor, they were forming a new national organization.

SDS faced the identical problem at the end of the 1960s with the Progressive Labor party (PL). Essentially what PL did was to caucus beforehand, to adopt tactics for promoting its line within a larger and more diffuse organization, and then, without any interest in what others might have to say, ramming through its predecided resolutions. After a season of hateful harangues and organizational division, very little remained.

Some Occupiers may respond, "But we're not trying to take over anything! We only want to be able to follow our own consciences!" Sadly, though, the impact of Marxist-Leninist vanguardism and unrestrained individualism on a larger body of variegated protesters may be pretty much the same. In each case there may be a fixed belief that one knows the Truth and has correctly determined What Is To Be Done, which makes it an unnecessary waste of time to Listen To The Experience Of Others. Those who hold these attitudes are likely to act in a way that will wound or even destroy the larger Movement that gives them a platform.

In the period between Seattle in 1999 and September 11, 2001, many activists were into a pattern of behavior that might unkindly be described as summit-hopping. Two young men from Chicago who had been in Seattle stayed in our basement for a night on their way to the next encounter with globalization in Quebec. I was struck by the fact that, as they explained themselves, when they came back to Chicago from Seattle they had been somewhat at a loss about what to do next. As each successive summit (Quebec, Genoa, Cancun) presented itself, they expected to be off to confront the Powers That Be in a new location, leaving in suspended state whatever beginnings they were nurturing in their local communities. So far as an outsider like myself could discern, there did not seem to be a long-term strategy directed toward creating an "*otro mundo*," a qualitatively new society.

This brings me to the forthcoming confrontation in Chicago in May. My wife Alice and I were living in Chicago in 1968. I was arrested and briefly jailed. Although many in the Movement considered the Chicago events to be a great victory, I believe it is the consensus of historians that the national perception of what happened in Chicago contributed to Nixon's victory in the November 1968 election. More important, as some of us foresaw these predominantly Northern activists like their SNCC predecessors appeared to have great difficulty in picking up again the slow work of "accompanying" in local communities.

I dread the possibility of a re-run of this sequence of events in 2012.

III

It may seem to some readers that "Staughton is once again pushing his nonviolence rap." However, although I am concerned that small groups in the Occupy Movement may contribute to unnecessary violence in Chicago, it is not violence as such that most worries me.

While I have all my life been personally committed to nonviolence, I have never attempted to impose this personal belief on movements in which I took part. Perhaps this is because as an historian I perceive certain situations for which I have not been able to imagine a nonviolent resolution.

The most challenging of these is slavery. At the time of the American Revolution there were about 600,000 slaves in the British colonies that became the United States. In the Civil War, more than 600,000 Union and Confederate soldiers were killed. It was literally true that, as President Lincoln put it in his Second Inaugural Address, every drop of blood drawn by the lash had to be "sunk" (repaid) by a drop of blood drawn by the sword.

Similarly, I cannot imagine telling Zapatistas that they should not be prepared to defend themselves if attacked by the Mexican army or paramilitaries. I believe that self-defense in these circumstances meets the criteria for a "just" use of violence set out by Archbishop Oscar Romero of El Salvador in his Pastoral Letters.

My fundamental concern is that the rhetoric of the Occupy Movement includes two propositions in tension with each other. We appear to say, on the one hand, that we must seek consensus, but on the other hand, that once a General Assembly is over individuals and grouplets are free to do their own thing.

A careful distinction is required. In general I endorse the idea of individuals or small groups carrying out actions that the group as a whole has not, or has not yet, endorsed. I believe that such actions are like experiments. Everyone involved, those who act and those who closely observe, learns from experiences of this kind. Indeed I have compared what happens in such episodes to the parable of the Sower in the New Testament. We are the seeds. We may be cast onto stony soil, on earth that lends itself only to thistles, or into fertile ground. Whatever our separate experiences, we must lay aside the impulse to defend our prowess as organizers and periodically pool our new knowledge, bad as well as good, so as to learn from each other and better shape a common strategy.

The danger I see is that rather than conceptualizing small group actions as a learning process, in the manner I have tried to describe, we might drift into the premature conclusion that nonviolence and consensus-seeking are for the General Assembly, but once we are out on the street sterner methods are required.

We have a little more than two months before Chicago in May. Unlike Seattle, the folks on the other side will not be unprepared. On January 18, the Chicago City Council overwhelmingly passed two ordinances pushed by [Mayor Rahm] Emanuel that restrict protest rules and expand the mayor's power to police the summits. Among other things, they increase fines for violating parade rules, allow the city to deputize police officers from outside Chicago for temporary duty and change the requirements for obtaining protest permits. Large signs and banners must now be approved, sidewalk protests require a permit, and permission for "large parades" will only be granted to those with a $1 million liability insurance policy. These are permanent changes in city law.

"Managing Dissent in Chicago," *In These Times*, March 2012, p. 7. It would be tragic if we failed to make good use of the precious period of time before all this must be confronted.

IV

So what do I recommend? I am eighty-two and no longer able to practice some of what I preach, but for what they may be worth, here are some responses to that question.

We need to act within a wide strategic context, and engage in more than tactical exercises.

We need to invite local people to join our ranks and institutions. We cannot hope to win the trust of others, especially others different from ourselves in class background, cultural preferences, race, or gender, unless we stay long enough to win that trust one day at a time. We must be prepared to spend years in communities where there may not be many fellow radicals.

In thinking about our own lives, and how we can contribute over what Nicaraguans call a "long trajectory," we need to acquire skills that poor and oppressed persons perceive to be needed.

We should understand consensus and nonviolence not as rigid rules, or as boundaries never to be crossed, but as a core or center from which our common actions radiate. Consensus is not just a style of conducting meetings. It seeks to avoid the common human tendency to say, after an action that runs into trouble, "I told you so." The practice of consensus envisions that discussion should continue until every one in the circle is prepared to proceed with a group decision. Perhaps different ones of us have varying degrees of enthusiasm or even serious apprehensions. Anyone who has such misgivings should voice his or her concern because it may be an issue that needs to be addressed. But we must talk things out to a point where as a group we can say, "We are doing this together."

Likewise nonviolence is under some circumstances the most promising way of challenging authority. Trotsky describes in his history of the Russian Revolution how, on International Women's Day, 1917, hundreds of women in St. Petersburg left their work in textile factories demanding Peace and Bread. The women confronted the Cossacks, the policemen on horseback, in the streets. Unarmed, the women approached the riders, saying in effect: "We have the same interests you do. Our husbands and sons are no different from yourselves. Don't ride us down!" And the Cossacks repeatedly refused to charge.

After all, policemen and correctional officers are also part of the 99 percent. When I visit prisoners at the supermaximum security prison in Youngstown, more than one officer has called out, "Remember me, Staughton? I used to be your client." When they could not find other work in our depressed city, which has the highest rate of poverty in the United States, many former steelworkers and truck drivers took prison jobs.

Nelson Mandela befriended a guard at Robben Island whose particular assignment was to watch over him. The officer, James Gregory, has written a book about it sub-titled *Nelson Mandela: My Prisoner, My Friend.* Mr. Gregory had a seat near the front at Mr. Mandela's inauguration.

The same logic applies to soldiers in a volunteer army. Thus one Occupier has written, "A thoughtful soldier, a soldier with a conscience, is the 1%'s worst nightmare." *The Occupy Wall Street Journal*, Nov. 2011, p. 2

In the end, I think, consensus decision-making and nonviolence both have to do with building a community of trust. One of my most chilling memories is to have heard a national officer of SDS talk to a large public meeting in Chicago about "icing" and "offing" persons with whom one disagreed. Actual murder of political comrades apparently took place in El Salvador, the United States, and, so I am told, Ireland.

Everything depends on whether two persons who differ about what should next be done nevertheless trust each other to proceed within the invisible boundaries of their common commitment.

A principal lesson of the 1960s is that maintenance and nurturing of that kind of trust becomes more difficult as a movement or organization grows larger. Here the Zapatistas have something to teach us. They do have a form of representative government in that delegates from different villages are elected to attend coordinating assemblies. But all governing is done within the cultural context of the ancient Mayan practice of "*mandar obediciendo*," that is, governing in obedience to those who are represented. Thus, after the uprising of January 1, 1994 negotiations began with emissaries from the national government. If a question arose as to which the Zapatista delegates were not instructed, they informed their counterparts that they had to go back to the villages for directio

All this lies down the road. For the moment, let's remind ourselves of the sentiment attributed by Charles Payne to residents working with SNCC in the Mississippi Delta half a century ago: they understood that "maintaining a sense of community was itself an act of resistance."

Staughton Lynd

Conclusion

Staughton Lynd can be described as a Quaker influenced by Marxism. Early in their marriage, Staughton and Alice lived on a commune in the Southern state of Georgia. From 1961-64, Staughton taught history at Atlanta's Spelman College, a college for black women. Moreover, in Freedom Summer of 1964 he served the cause of civil rights as the coordinator of the Mississippi Freedom Schools.

Thanks in part to the efforts of historian Edmund Morgan, Staughton and family moved to New Haven, Connecticut and Staughton joined Yale's history department. At this Ivy League university he made history. A pacifist and conscientious objector, the untenured Professor Lynd, along with Tom Hayden and Communist historian Herbert Aptheker, visited Hanoi in 1965 during the Vietnam War. As a result, he was blacklisted at Yale and by the American academy.

Staughton responded by forming a new professional identity. He earned a law degree from the University of Chicago and devoted himself to social justice as an attorney. Alice became a draft counselor and a paralegal.

In 1976 the Lynds moved to the rust belt in Youngstown, Ohio, where they continue to reside. As an act of "accompaniment" with the poor and dispossessed, they have served the distressed working class in the heart of a de-industrialized America. Alice enrolled at the University of Pittsburgh to get her own law degree, and then joined her husband as a full partner. Their strenuous efforts to stop steel-mill closings and to protect the benefits of displaced workers and retirees were epic.

Since their retirement in 1996, Staughton and Alice have focused their legal struggles against the injustice of the American criminal justice system. Witness their efforts in regard to the 1993 Lucasville, Ohio prison rebellion. According to historian Howard Zinn, Staughton's book *Lucasville* "is one of the most powerful indictments of our 'justice system' I have ever read. What comes across is a litany of flaws deep in the system, and recognizably not unique to Lucasville."

Well done, Staughton and Alice.

Selected Bibliography

Writings by Staughton Lynd

Anti-Federalism in Dutchess County, New York: A Study of Democracy and Class Conflict in the Revolutionary Era. Chicago: Loyola University Press, 1962.

Class Conflict, Slavery, and the United States Constitution: Ten Essays. New ed., Cambridge University Press, 2009).

The Fight against Shutdowns: Youngstown Steel Mill Closings. San Pedro: Singlejack Books, 1982.

Homeland: Oral Histories of Palestine and Palestinians. [with Sam Bahour and Alice Lynd] New York: Olive Branch Press, 1994.

Intellectual Origins of American Radicalism. New ed., Cambridge University Press, 2009 *Labor Law for the Rank and Filer, or, Building Solidarity while Staying Clear of the Law.*
Chicago: Charles H. Kerr Publishers, 1994.

Living Inside Our Hope: A Steadfast Radical's Thoughts on Rebuilding the Movement. Ithaca, NY: Cornell University/ILR Press, 1997.

Lucasville: The Untold Story of a Prison Uprising. New ed., with Foreward by Mumia Abu Jamal. Oakland, CA: PM Press, 2011.

The New Rank and File. [with Alice Lynd] Ithaca: ILR Press, 2000.

Nonviolence in America: A Documentary History. [with Alice Lynd] Rev. ed. Maryknoll, NY: Orbis Books, 1995.

The Other Side. [with Tom Hayden] New York: New American Library, 1967.

Rank and File: Personal Histories by Working Class Organizers. [with Alice Lynd] New and expanded ed., Chicago: Haymarket Books, 2011.

The Resistance. [with Michael Ferber] Boston: Beacon Press, 1971.

Stepping Stones: Memoir of a Life Together. [with Alice Lynd] Lanham, MD: Lexington Books, 2009.

Strategy and Power: Two Essays toward a New American Socialism. [with Gar Alperovitz] Boston: Beacon Press, 1973.

"We Are All Leaders": The Alternative Unionism of the Early 1930s: The Working Class in American History. Urbana, Ill.: University of Illinois Press, 1996.

Wobblies and Zapatistas: Conversations on Anarchism, Marxism and Radical History. [with Andrej Grubacic] Oakland: PM Press, 2008.